THE CREATOR
REVOLUTION

THE CREATOR REVOLUTION

HOW TODAY'S CREATIVE TALENTS ARE SHAPING OUR TOMORROW

CATHERINE YEO

NEW DEGREE PRESS

THE CREATOR REVOLUTION

How Today's Creative Talents Are Shaping Our Tomorrow

ISBN   979-8-88504-062-4   *Paperback*

979-8-88504-617-6   *Kindle Ebook*

979-8-88504-167-6   *Ebook*

For more information, please visit

www.catherinehyeo.com/creator

To everyone out there with

a *story* that needs to be told,

a *voice* that needs to be heard

"Fill your paper with the breathings of your heart."

—WILLIAM WORDSWORTH

CONTENTS

Introduction

Jenna never imagined she could achieve her creative dreams. Now, she is a dance YouTuber with tens of millions of views.

In high school, Jenna thought her future would entail being a doctor or lawyer, careers commonly associated and stereotyped with Asian Americans. Even though she dreamed of being a performer, Jenna never saw representation for Asian Americans beyond those two careers in her home state of Iowa.

Everything changed after she watched a K-pop (South Korean pop) video online.

Suddenly, Jenna saw someone who looked like her perform. She realized she could break free from the mold she thought she had to fit into.

Mesmerized by that one K-pop video, she taught herself how to dance by watching tutorials on YouTube and mimicking the movements in the reflection of her bedroom's glass door. With her newfound inspiration and skills, she began to dance spontaneously in public. Her sister filmed her dancing in front of The Bean, a massive tourist hot spot in Chicago. She didn't care when tourists walked by or stopped to point at her—she just kept dancing. The video was then uploaded to YouTube, where many of her future dances would find their home, and it went viral.

Jenna's journey, which we will discuss in more detail in Chapter 9, is a story of self-initiation that can happen to anyone. The power of online content has reached such heights a young girl in Iowa saw a video from South Korea, which inspired her to learn how to dance and post content, which in turn inspired millions of others. That would not have been possible even just twenty years ago. Our society has progressed to a stage where any piece of online content now has the power to greatly impact anyone in the world, for better or for worse.

The internet was developed in the second half of the twentieth century. Digital content has been a natural output of its existence, ranging anywhere from adorable kitten videos to fanfiction, educational podcasts to NFTs (non-fungible tokens). According to the venture capital firm SignalFire, more than 50 million people around the world identified as a creator in 2020. In the United States, the most desired job for children aged eight to twelve is not that of an astronaut, or even an athlete—instead, they want to be YouTubers (Dzhanova, 2019).

Business intelligence tool Domo discovered that on average, in a single minute on the internet in 2021,

- YouTube viewers watched 694 thousand hours of videos combined.
- Facebook users shared 240 thousand photos.
- TikTok viewers watched 167 million videos.
- Twitter users posted 575 thousand tweets.
- Discord communities and users sent 668 thousand messages.

Despite the glowing statistics, many people in our society still do not accept content creating as a "real" career. Creative industries as a whole are often not accepted or respected as a path to stability. The novelty and ambiguity of digital content creation have added another layer of misconception and skepticism to the mix.

These skeptics are overlooking a new reality: digital creators are fundamentally changing the way our society operates.

In 2014, high school me—very much a nerdy fangirl of large franchises like *Harry Potter* and *Star Wars*—began to publish fanfiction and fan art online for fun. Slowly, I built an online audience of hundreds of thousands of strangers around the world, enough so I was earning money from my writing and art before my sixteenth birthday.

Before I became a creator, I was an avid content consumer. I have been watching YouTube for over a decade, and even today I spend at least one hour a day almost without fail following my favorite YouTube creators. I stay up to date on news and trends by reading my favorite writers on platforms like Substack and Mirror, I listen to podcasts on Spotify on long walks, and I follow Twitch streamers' invigorating gameplay and stories when I fold laundry. Consuming content has become an essential component of my daily routine.

As a creator, I've worked with a variety of content formats, topics, and platforms. I published my writing and art online, first on fiction platforms like AO3 and Wattpad, then on independent writing platforms such as Medium, and last on broader social media. While writing this book, I experimented with creator platforms I never dared to publicly post content on before, like TikTok, LinkedIn, and Substack, to begin building my book audience. I was a creator long before I understood what a "creator" was or who qualified as one.

After years of learning as a creator and observing the landscape, I want to share the stories behind why the Creator Revolution emerged as a possibility and present a vision of the future our society is transforming toward. *The Creator Revolution* examines the rise and impact of digital content creators and how they are revolutionizing the ways our society operates.

This book will first and foremost be for *anyone* who consumes content and aspires to create content. You will learn about the technological evolution that has led to the rise of digital creators, how to prepare for the changes the Creator Revolution is bringing, and how to step into the shoes of a creator. This book is most suitable for Generation Z, the first generation to be born into a world of digital content, but *its audience goes beyond one generation*: as we will see throughout the stories woven throughout the book, content creation is for individuals of all ages and backgrounds.

Failing to understand what is going on will leave you far behind in a pivotal moment in history that will affect every aspect of your daily life, from earning money to buying groceries to even fixing your toilet. By being a creator, or consuming content from other creators, you will also find you can create new opportunities for yourself.

This book is divided into three sections:

- Part I, **"Societal Shifts,"** illustrates the rise of creators and examines how content creation is transforming the future of work, commerce, education, and media.
- Part II, **"Self-Made Success,"** focuses on different methods by which creators are revolutionizing themselves, such as opening new doors, building their own businesses, and creating representation in media.
- Part III, **"Challenges and Opportunities,"** explores issues creators currently face and proposes potential solutions to address them.

Over the course of this book, you will read stories of long-established creators such as Michelle Phan, beauty creator turned multi-million-dollar makeup empire leader; Issa Rae, star and co-creator of HBO's award-winning television series *Insecure*, who launched her filmmaking career on YouTube; and Jimmy "MrBeast" Donaldson, a creator and philanthropist with over 230 million followers across social media.

At the same time, you will also hear from creators across a range of backgrounds and audiences, including Schuyler Bailar, an Instagram educator of queer resources and social justice issues; Claudine James, an English teacher who went from teaching twenty-two students in her classroom to over three million students on TikTok; and Nastassia Ponomarenko, a fitness creator who has been financially independent since age seventeen and has since founded three businesses. Furthermore, you will hear from pioneering experts such as Li Jin, the venture capitalist who coined the term "passion economy," and read about companies that have transformed the creator landscape, such as Patreon, TikTok, and Roblox.

Creators are both our present and our future. I'm excited to have you join me on this journey to learn more together. Get ready to learn more about the birth and explosion of digital content that has already begun to transform every corner of our world.

Welcome to the Creator Revolution.

CHAPTER 1

Creators Unveiled

"Be brave enough to live life creatively. The creative place where no one else has ever been."

—ALAN ALDA, ACTOR AND COMEDIAN

Like many other high school kids, Imane Anys was obsessed with playing video games.

After falling in love with the video game *League of Legends*, seventeen-year-old Imane joined livestreaming website Twitch in search of more gaming friends and teammates. She began to stream on the site, gradually gaining a following for her competitive gameplay and energetic personality.

By the time Imane started college, burdened with an intense chemical engineering workload, streaming had become a part-time job for her. On Twitch, she received small donations and monthly subscriptions, the most common tier costing only five dollars a month. Rainbow-written usernames of her donors filled the whiteboard behind her in her dorm room.

It was enough to chip away at her student loans, which had amounted to over twenty thousand dollars. By her second year of college, Imane was able to pay off half of her student loans in just one month from Twitch donations and sponsorships (D'Anastasio, 2021). It was no longer merely a hobby, or even a part-time job anymore—it was a full-fledged career brimming with limitless opportunity. After breaking into the top 100 most-followed streamers on the site, she dropped out the next year to pursue Twitch fulltime.

Unlike most gamers, Imane turned her love for video games into a fulltime career creating content about her greatest passion. Since then, she has also co-founded OfflineTV, a content creator collective, built a large merch brand, and appeared in a 20th Century Studios film. Now with over 9 million followers on Twitch and 600 million views on YouTube, Imane—better known by her online alias "Pokimane"—is a household name in the gaming world.

Imane's story is the epitome of the creator spirit: anyone can be a creator. What started out as a hobby drastically changed the trajectory of her life and jumpstarted her career as one of the most popular gaming streamers in history. Creators can come from the most unexpected corners. There is no limit on who can be a creator, what content creators can make, and how they go about doing it.

• • •

In an increasingly digitized society, Imane's story is only one of millions of incredible journeys of digital content creators. But first, we must take a step back to pinpoint what exactly a digital content creator is.

Digital content broadly encapsulates any content that is published on the internet. Most often this takes the form of one of the five categories I have classified: video, audio, images, text, and experiences.

1. **Video**: Video blogs ("vlogs"), short-form videos, music videos, video livestreams, online courses, etc.
2. **Audio**: Music, podcasts, etc.
3. **Images**: Artwork, photos, infographics, etc.
4. **Text**: Blog posts, fanfiction, newsletters, tweets, poetry, etc.
5. **Experiences**: Communities (groups that actively share information around a common interest, topic, or characteristic), games, virtual concerts, digital fashion shows, etc.

While defining digital content seems straightforward, given the novelty and ever-changing atmosphere around this phenomenon, the term "creator" is inherently difficult to define in an all-encompassing and consistent style.

Li Jin, the founder and managing partner of Atelier Ventures, a fund that focuses on investing in creator-related start-ups, defines a creator broadly but emphasizes the importance of having an audience. "A creator is anyone who has built up an audience on digital platforms," she wrote in her blog.

Others have a different perspective. Sahil Lavingia is the co-founder and CEO of Gumroad, an e-commerce platform where creators can sell digital products, such as e-books, online courses, and memberships, directly to consumers (Finley, 2020). Founded in 2011, Gumroad used a more specific conceptualization of creators. The company considered a creator to be "someone who creates art and would create more art if they had more time [and] money," Sahil recalled in a tweet.

In this book, we will define a **digital content creator** as an individual who makes and publishes digital content consistently and has built up an online audience. From this point onward, anytime we refer to "content" or "creators," we will only be referring to digital content and digital content creators.

The word "creator" is not new. According to the Online Etymology Dictionary, it originates from the Latin word *creare*, which means "to make or bring forth." However, its association with online content dates back to the early 2010s, when YouTube sought a new term to refer to its top stars (Lorenz, 2019). Wanting a term more concise than "YouTube stars" and more fitting than "partners," they found the perfect word: *creators*. As more individuals around the world embarked on their own YouTube journey, the word **creator** became mainstream.

Today, "creators" captures far more than YouTubers. Digital content spans video, audio, images, text, experiences, and other potential mediums, and so do digital content creators. A teenager who publishes photos of their home cooking on Instagram is a creator; a mother who writes blog posts on Blogspot about gardening and home decor is a creator; Imane, who publishes videos and livestreams of her gameplay and commentary, is also a creator.

In her blog, Li identifies five criteria that define a creator, namely the first five elements on the list below. Here I elaborate on her criteria and add two important elements in order to embrace the complexity and broaden the discussion of who fits under the umbrella of "creators":

1. **Content Creation:** At its most literal level, creators need to *create* something of any form of digital content.

2. **Audience Aspiration:** Creators want to grow an audience who follows and believes in their work, even if they don't currently have an audience today. Some proponents have advocated for a definition of "creator" to even embrace those who create but never share their creation(s) with

others, but I see growing a digital audience as a pivotal element of being a creator.

3. **Value:** Creators need to generate value (in the broadest sense) for their audience, creating something impactful or useful for others. Their audience must be able to identify tangible value in the content they create.

4. **Intentionality:** Publishing one Tweet or posting occasional life milestones on Facebook does not automatically make you a creator. Creators need to be intentional about their craft and strive to improve their content and augment their growth.

5. **Inclination:** Creators want to create more if they are given further resources, especially time and money.

6. **Consistency:** Creators should aim to publish digital content consistently (or on a frequent-enough basis) so they have the ability to grow an audience. The work must exceed a one-time endeavor. This criterion goes hand-in-hand with intentionality.

7. **Independence:** The scope of this book is limited to content created by independent creators and individuals, so large organizations like news publications, Hollywood production studios, universities, etc. will be excluded from discussion.

To see how this applies in action, we can see how Alisha Wielfaert satisfies all these defined criteria as a creator in the case study at the end of this chapter (more details shown in Table 1.1).

CREATOR TIP:
What kind of value can I offer my audience?

There are three main categories of value you, as a creator, can best provide. Choose one to begin with, and create your content with that value in mind.

- **Entertainment**

  Examples:
  - Comedy skits intended to make people laugh.
  - Art pieces that awe anyone who comes across them.
  - Short films with suspenseful storytelling designed to enthrall your audience.

- **Education**

  Examples:
  - Courses that share knowledge and insights on how to manage one's finances.
  - Newsletters that provide valuable fashion tips.
  - Active, tight-knit communities that provide support and discussion around a specific topic.

- **Inspiration**

  Examples:
  - Vlogs that share anecdotes about juggling a full-time career with a family, inspiring your audience to understand more about such a lifestyle.
  - Short-form videos that demonstrate your cooking process, encouraging your audience to try cooking new dishes.
  - A study blog that displays pictures of your colorful handwritten notes, inspiring your audience to create organized notes and advance their academic studies.

Throughout this book, we'll encounter the stories of many individuals who have been labeled as content creators—either by themselves or by others—across a wide variety of platforms and niches. One such individual, Caitlin Lam, is a freelance designer who has accumulated over 125 thousand followers and 3.5 million views on TikTok (@caitlinnlam) for her art and graphic design videos. Despite her success and large audience, Caitlin doesn't consider herself a creator. Instead, she primarily sees her content as a "traffic guide" to her freelance business, funneling her audience to her design business so companies, shops, and individuals can pay for her designs and branding work. Some others have progressed past the term "creator" to adopt terms such as "content entrepreneur" or the phrase "small business owner," which better reflect the entrepreneurial nature of controlling and earning money from one's content (which we will probe deeper in Chapters 7 and 8).

Thus, it's important to recognize "creator" isn't a perfect, one-size-fits-all term, and the role continues to evolve with each passing day. To examine that evolution, in the next chapter, we will begin by examining and answering a key question: what economic needs and technological advancements enabled the rise of creators?

A creator is any individual who publishes digital content consistently and has built up an audience on platforms online. Anyone can be a creator.

When Alisha Wielfaert realized coaching was her life calling, she quit her corporate sales job to launch her own business. Even though she desired to spend all her time conducting one-on-one coaching, she quickly realized being an entrepreneur didn't work like that. Instead, she needed to also be a creator.

"To grow your business, I know your email list is the most valuable thing you have when you're in online marketing and online sales. So everything points toward 1) how can I serve that email list I currently have, and 2) how can I build my email list going forward," Alisha reflected. She turned to content creation as the answer to both questions.

While private coaching remained the foundation of her business, Alisha recognized the importance of scaling her reach and impact to larger audiences. She decided to experiment with various forms of content to determine which mediums were the most valuable.

Alisha tapped into traditional social media platforms such as Instagram and LinkedIn to share her learnings and insights about positive psychology and leadership. Her knowledge was then repurposed and expanded upon on her blog and in her weekly podcast. These content mediums helped her accomplish both of her goals: serving her existing audience and growing her reach to new potential clients (across different media platforms and formats too).

To supplement her private coaching, Alisha experimented with live courses, which helped her reach and instruct new customers as well as determine what people are most interested in learning from her. Having recorded these courses, she packaged her teachings into online courses sold on Kajabi, an all-in-one digital course marketplace. Not only did these courses bring her a steady passive income, they also directed new clients to one-on-one coaching appointments if a course customer desired more after the course ended.

The most important piece of content Alisha focuses on is the community she cultivates. "I create sacred space in a digital way," she remarked. Using private Facebook groups, she ensures her audience feels seen and heard, equipping them with the ability to engage with each other and herself directly at any time.

Within a few years, Alisha blossomed from a corporate salesperson to a budding creator and thriving entrepreneur. Starting from zero followers across the board, she has since amassed 6,000 followers across her email list and social media as well as 30,000 podcast downloads.

Content	Alisha created online courses, blog posts, social media posts, a podcast, and communities.
Audience Aspiration	Alisha's primary goal is to grow her email list.
Value	Alisha's content focuses on sharing insights about positive psychology, leadership, and creativity, which are the main topics and values of her private coaching business.
Intentionality	Alisha carefully crafts her content to serve her existing community and further build her audience.
Inclination	Alisha always wants to create more content, which is why she continues to experiment with different formats and mediums.
Consistency	Though it may differ across her content mediums, Alisha sets a schedule for each content form. For example, she publishes a podcast episode every week.
Independence	Alisha is an independent creator.

Table 1.1: How Alisha satisfies the seven criteria for being a creator.

PART I:

SOCIETAL SHIFTS

In Part I, "Societal Shifts," we will explore what led to the rise of creators and examine the important transformations that are taking shape during this new era.

Chapter 2 introduces the notion of the passion economy. The chapter dives into how the passion economy innovated upon the gig economy to usher in a groundbreaking new economic system.

Chapter 3 defines what an influencer is and reveals how influencers have transformed how we buy and sell products today.

Chapter 4 illustrates how knowledge creators offer a new form of education. The chapter also acknowledges and looks at how education from knowledge creators can propagate misinformation.

Chapter 5 showcases stories of creators who have transformed the media landscape, particularly in fictional entertainment and news journalism.

CHAPTER 2

The Economic Evolution

"We are born with eyes not just to see beauty, but to find it. We are born with hands not just to hold beauty, but to create it. Don't just sit there. Find and create. In others, in the world, in yourself."

—C. JOYBELL C., AUTHOR

When I was twelve, I liked to spend my free time curled up in bed dreaming about fictional universes such as Hogwarts and a galaxy far, far away.

My fanatical interest grew to the point where I began to map out my own visions of those worlds. These visions turned into fanfiction and fan art, in which I investigated the effects of different plot decisions, designed new characters, and rewrote storylines to be set in alternate realities or universes.

What was special about the fandom ecosystem, especially with large franchises like *Harry Potter* and *Star Wars*, was it came with a massive network of support built in: fans of the fandom itself. They were equally (or more) invested in the same interests as I was, and we shared any nugget of our imagination to celebrate our collective passions. I began building a following by sharing my writing and art on social media platforms where fandom bases had a presence such as Tumblr and Twitter. I also made new friends with fellow writers and artists, some of whom I've met in person and still talk to today.

As I continued to post my stories and artwork throughout the mid- to late-2010s, I started to accept requests for custom storylines or specific art pieces. My following grew from hundreds to thousands to hundreds of thousands. They appreciated a creator who heeded their requests and feedback, and we were all bonded by our love for the fandoms we were a part of.

Fans began to recognize me for my distinctive style of writing and art. With the increase in requests, many of which have surpassed the topics of fandom to generic prompts, I was slower to fulfill them. To my surprise, one follower asked if she could pay for her customized request if I completed hers quicker. I was bewildered—someone trusted an internet stranger so much they were willing to pay me? I quickly agreed and set up a PayPal account to accept her payment.

I happily fulfilled her request, thinking it was a one-time occurrence. Then, tips and donations poured in from long-time supporters who admired my work. I received more commission requests, some as small as a flash fiction story, some as large as an art piece they wanted to frame and hang on their walls.

My bank balance had started at zero. It climbed to three digits within a month and only grew from there.

To my fifteen-year-old self who was writing and drawing on the internet for fun, it was unfathomable I could make money online through my creative works. Even more unimaginable was the number itself.

My creator story is not unique. A 2017 study led by Robert Shapiro, the former US Under Secretary of Commerce for Economic Affairs, revealed nearly seventeen million Americans earned income posting their personal creations on nine platforms (Amazon Publishing, eBay, Etsy, Instagram, Shapeways, Tumblr, Twitch, WordPress, and YouTube). Five years have passed since; today, not only has the number of platforms on which creators can exist exploded, but so has the number of creators and the amount of income made from their creations. I expect all of these metrics will only continue to rise, all around the world.

We live in a new era where it is possible for creators to make money online through their creative endeavors. In Part I of this book, "Societal Shifts," we will learn about the critical transformations that are taking shape during this new era. We begin by examining the economic evolution creators have ushered in.

THE GIG ECONOMY

Prior to the emergence of the Creator Revolution, we witnessed the transformative rise of the gig economy.

In a **gig economy**, large numbers of individuals engaged in part-time work and were paid on a task-by-task basis. Marketplaces used digital tools to automate the matching of supply and demand by connecting freelancers with customers to provide quick services for the customer while offering short-term independent employment for the freelancers. Their technology effectively erased hurdles for both the freelancer and the marketplace. Because of the nature of part-time contracts, the provider could easily find employees through the general public, while the freelancer could focus on the service task at hand now that customer acquisition and pricing were handled by the platforms.

Essentially, the gig economy successfully created more flexible, two-sided labor markets that previously did not exist. Such marketplaces—including ride-sharing apps (e.g.

Uber, Lyft, Grab), food or grocery delivery apps (e.g. Door-Dash, Instacart, FoodPanda), and asset-sharing services (e.g. Airbnb, Turo) flourished and offered a path to self-employment for millions of individuals.

Despite the gig economy inherently offering flexible employment opportunities, it lacked the ability to guarantee consistent income. Because demand for services varied from day to day, sometimes even hour to hour, earnings would arrive in unpredictable bursts, with a large percentage of those earnings going to the marketplace platforms themselves. In a viral TikTok video he uploaded in 2021, food delivery driver Smithson Michael tearfully shared, "I just spent an hour driving around for a 1.19-dollar tip…I got a 1.19-dollar tip and two dollars from the app. What's that? That's not even enough to cover gas. *How am I supposed to survive like that?*"

Furthermore, the structure of the gig economy institutionalized every service worker and flattened their individuality. Every job was standardized, and these platforms didn't care about each worker's strengths, interests, and personality. The top priority was always to complete the assigned task as quickly and consistently as possible. "While the promise was 'Be your own boss,' the work was often one-dimensional," venture capitalist Li Jin, who we briefly heard from in Chapter 1, wrote in a 2019 essay. "Gig work isn't going anywhere. But there are now more ways to capitalize on creativity."

THE PASSION ECONOMY

In 2019, Li coined the term "**passion economy**" to describe the phenomenon of how individuals, especially content creators, could now monetize their individuality and hobbies through unique, creative work.

The emergence of the gig economy offered individuals the opportunity to take up temporary, one-time jobs using digital services like ride-sharing and food delivery apps. While gig work customers varied day to day, a creator could build a loyal audience and maintain a higher level of consistency. On top of that unique advantage, the passion economy takes the flexibility the gig economy provides to an extreme: creators have full autonomy over their time, business model, and services or goods offered.

	Platform payment	Sponsored content	Paid subscriptions	Tips, gifts, & donations	In-app shopping
Facebook	Yes	Yes	Yes	Yes	Yes
Instagram	Yes	Yes	Yes	Yes	Yes
Pinterest	Yes	Yes	No	No	Yes
Reddit	No	Yes	No	Yes	No
Snapchat	Yes	Yes	No	Yes	No
TikTok	Yes	Yes	No	Yes	Yes
Tumblr	No	Yes	Yes	Yes	No
Twitch	Yes	Yes	Yes	Yes	No
Twitter	No	Yes	Yes	Yes	No
YouTube	Yes	Yes	Yes	Yes	Yes

Image 2.1: A list of social media platforms that allow creators to make money through a variety of different methods, such as receiving direct platform payments, posting sponsored content, earning paid subscriptions from fans, receiving tips/virtual gifts/donations, and offering in-app shopping.

A key component of the passion economy is the existence of creator platforms. **Creator platforms** grant creators the ability to distribute their content and build a following. Examples include many of the largest social media apps, such as YouTube, TikTok, Instagram, Twitter, and Pinterest.

But creator platforms certainly aren't limited to social networks. Blogging and newsletter sites (e.g. Blogspot, Revue, Substack), music sharing platforms (e.g. SoundCloud, Mixcloud), and virtual course offering marketplaces (e.g. Udemy, Teachable, Podia) are just some of the many platforms that exist for specific niches.

Once upon a time, artists, musicians, writers, and others with creative interests had a difficult time finding stable, full-time careers centered around their passions. With the rise of creator platforms, an age of creator empowerment dawned upon us. These paths range from traditional creator roles like YouTubers and podcasters, to video course instructors and virtual coaches. The topics are equally diverse, spanning common subjects like how to grow your own business to niche skills such as how to keep all your plants alive.

To supplement the value creator platforms provide, **creator tools** equip creators with more specific apparatuses for turning their passions into a business. They provide functionalities such as monetizing fan interactions, managing virtual communities, and automating content publishing schedules.

In 2021, *The Information* discovered over two billion dollars had been invested in start-ups building platforms and tools for creators in the first half of the year alone. That same year, global early-stage venture capital firm Antler found there are over 220 such businesses. These creator platforms and tools are revolutionary in three manners:

1. **They encourage individuality rather than stifle it.**
   Unlike traditional jobs that prioritize consistency, such as assembly line manufacturing or financial accounting,

individuality is a prized value for content creators. Recall from Chapter 1 the criteria of creators include Value, Audience Aspiration, and Intentionality. Creator platforms support individuals who provide a service only they themselves can create. These platforms encourage creators to lean into their individuality and highlight their diverse passions so users can experience and choose from a diverse range of content.

2. **They enable any individual to be a self-sustaining business.**

   Prior to the passion economy, making and maintaining a sustainable living through creative skills was mostly restricted to businesses and professional experts. Now, that ability has trickled down to the general public. Any individual can launch, operate, and grow a business that stems from their own self due to the many digital creator platforms and tools.

   For example, custom, personal websites used to be a complicated endeavor that required extensive design and coding. Now, an abundance of no-code website builders like Squarespace, Wix, and Bubble exist. When social platforms transitioned to dominate smartphones instead of laptops, mobile-first "link-in-bio" sites such as Beacons, Linktree, and Jemi emerged to give creators even more options.

   Furthermore, these platforms and tools generate revenue by either taking a percentage of the creator's earnings or charging a standard price for usage of their services. Unlike gig economy marketplaces, which seek to promote as many one-time transactions as possible, creator platforms and tools are by nature incentivized to help creators succeed and flourish as a business (which we will examine further in Chapter 8).

3. **They focus on selling digital products and services.**
   Online shopping platforms like Amazon, Shopee, Etsy,
   Shopify, and eBay all primarily focus on selling physical
   products. Gig economy marketplaces like Uber, Door-
   Dash, and TaskRabbit built their business models around
   in-person services.

   Creator platforms are different. The passion economy
   is about offering something differentiated and growing
   your audience around it, and that "something" is not
   required to be a physical product or an in-person service. Instead, creator platforms spotlight digital products.
   Past generations of knowledge "creators" (which we will
   learn more about in Chapter 4) could only reach regional
   customers by teaching in-person classes; now, anyone can
   offer video courses and webinars on platforms like Kajabi,
   Teachable, and Podia. Previously, the primary method of
   selling written content was through publishing books,
   which is a slow and arduous process; now, anyone can
   publish writing and earn money from it on digital platforms like Substack, Medium, and Wattpad.

There are numerous paths to monetization in the passion
economy once individuals leverage their individuality and
interests. According to *Forbes*, over two million fulltime creators worldwide earned at least six-figure incomes in 2020, a
figure that's bound to continue to rise.

Despite the clear potential of success, many still believe
being a creator is not a real career. One individual who has
continuously faced these doubts is Australian fitness YouTuber Chloe Ting. Now sitting with over 21 million subscribers
and 2.5 billion views, she started her career not as a creator,
but in the world of finance.

Chloe graduated with a bachelor's degree in economics & business statistics, a Master of Philosophy, and earned First Class Honors in econometrics. After graduation, she worked as an actuarial analyst at a corporation for over three years. In her free time, she liked to make videos for fun. However, her boss at the time told her to choose between her job and her after-hours hobby, because "it was a distraction." So, she decided to quit her stable, corporate job and begin her YouTube career, uploading and creating videos about fashion, travel, and makeup.

Her parents were furious, thinking it was a waste of her degree. Even her most supportive friends thought she was crazy and "too old to be on YouTube and social media" at twenty-nine. While she considered her job to be fulltime, no one else did. Instead, she was told she should go have children and live responsibly.

The harsh skepticism extended beyond her circle of family and friends. Whenever she told someone she was a YouTuber, they replied with comments like "That's not a real job" and "YouTuber…do you make any money?" In her 2019 VidCon talk, she recalled seeing a newspaper that had placed her in a headline as a prominent example of how to waste money.

She progressed from makeup tutorials to fitness videos, where she found her content niche—short, free workout videos and recipes to help people with their fitness journeys. Her first viral video was a ten-minute ab workout routine posted in 2016. Laying on a pink yoga mat in a gym studio, surrounded by walls of mirrors, Chloe guided her fans through different exercises. Her workout videos grew in popularity as other content creators tried them, with her viewership spiking during the COVID-19 quarantine, when gyms were forced to close amid lockdown and people searched for at-home workout solutions.

Chloe admits even years after she began her fulltime You-Tube career, many people still don't understand the content creator line of work. She remains hesitant in telling people what her occupation is, but she is very proud of being a creator and producing a positive impact for her audience. Being a content creator is very much a real career, and it's a pivotal piece of the growing passion economy.

Furthermore, it's an occupation with virtually limitless earning potential. Mint, a personal financial management website, revealed in 2021 that a YouTube video with one million views can earn up to five thousand dollars. According to *Forbes*, then nine-year-old YouTuber Ryan Kaji earned 30 million dollars in 2020 alone (and we'll learn more about Ryan's story in the following chapter).

Even if you have no desire to be a creator or have never touched YouTube in your life, it turns out the creator ecosystem is directly contributing and feeding into our society nevertheless—very much impacting *you*. According to an Oxford Economics report, the YouTube ecosystem contributed 16 billion dollars to the United States' total GDP in 2019; that amount supports the equivalent of 345,000 full-time jobs. A Boston Consulting Group whitepaper disclosed short-form videos generated a 193-billion-dollar economic footprint in 2020, directly resulting in roughly 659,000 new jobs.

The passion economy is about more than just creators. It is reshaping the landscape of work for everyone and alternating the fundamental underpinnings of our society right now.

RISE OF THE PASSION ECONOMY

While the internet has existed for decades, the development and growth of social networks in the last ten to twenty years are what have truly enabled the passion economy.

Previously, a seller created a product, which went through a supply chain before landing in a store, and a consumer bought the product. There was no communication between the creator and the consumer; the consumer enjoyed what they could find. The seller may have known how many units of an item had sold, but they had no idea what consumers thought about them beyond one-time reviews most consumers don't bother to write. Because they couldn't get real-time feedback from customers, the seller also could not easily tailor new products to what customers wanted.

Today, social networks such as Twitter, WhatsApp, and Instagram have achieved global reach and connected every fiber of the world digitally. It is now possible for a direct line of connection between the creator and the consumer to exist: the seller creates a product, the consumer expresses their enjoyment of the product, and it turns into a communication loop that encourages more interaction, product ideation, and product sales. Social platforms needed to be developed first so creators could find their fans (consumers), and fans in turn could find the creators they liked best.

These new integrated, interconnected platforms empowered individuals of all backgrounds and interests to monetize their individuality and creativity, giving rise to the passion economy.

Two individuals who realized the power of the interconnected internet were Sam Yam and Jack Conte. Both individuals with creative passions themselves, they used this revelation to build Patreon, one of the earliest and now largest tools for creator monetization.

Sam had played the piano at an elite level for over fifteen years, all the way to Carnegie Hall, the concert hall every musician aspires to play in one day (Yam, Jin, and Murrow, 2020). But he didn't see how he could turn his lifelong passion for music into a career. Out of nearly 150,000 Americans polled in 2020, the US Bureau of Labor Statistics found only 0.08 percent found employment as professional musicians or singers.

Jack was a musician, producer, and songwriter. Formed together with singer-songwriter and bassist Nataly Dawn, the duo known as Pomplamoose has been uploading musical covers and original songs to YouTube since 2008 (Wertheimer, 2010).

YouTube was founded in 2005 and has been pivotal in contributing to the birth of the passion economy, with creators such as Chloe Ting achieving great success on the platform. In their early days, however, YouTubers could not earn revenue—until the YouTube Partner Program was launched in December 2007. From then until the later 2010s, one could only make money on YouTube by meeting minimum metrics, joining the program, and then running ads on their videos to earn revenue.

Hundreds of millions of people loved and watched Pomplamoose's videos, but only a few hundred dollars from YouTube's ad revenue were making their way into Jack's bank account, nowhere near the cost of the videos. In his 2017 TED talk, Jack recalled how whenever he told people he was a musician, people instantly responded with a message of pity: "I hope you make it one day."

For Sam, it was incredible how someone could have no way to monetize a craft that had been honed for fifteen years and validated at the highest level. For Jack, this was happening in 2013—already eight years after YouTube's inception. While the passion economy was born, it wasn't ready to grow. The pipeline for creators to make money was irreparably broken.

Sam and Jack, former college roommates, set out to solve this problem for other artists and creators just like them. In 2013, they developed Patreon, a platform that allowed anyone to be a "patron" for creators. Each patron paid a set amount of money on a recurring basis or per piece of content. In return, they received benefits and perks such as bonus "exclusive" content, acknowledgments and shoutouts, physical rewards, and so on.

By 2022, according to the company's accumulated metrics, Patreon has given a platform to over 200 thousand creators, consisting of YouTubers, artists, writers, podcasters, musicians, educators, and other types of creators. They have been supported by more than six million patrons combined, and creators have earned over two billion dollars on the site alone. Creators who have leveraged Patreon successfully include Hollywood actress and writer Issa Rae (who we'll learn more about in Chapter 5), who joined Patreon in 2015 to fund her web series *The Misadventures of Awkward Black Girl* before creating *Insecure* on HBO, and the Try Guys (who we will revisit in Chapter 8), who used Patreon to fund their own independent media company (Tseng, 2021).

Today, Patreon's homepage tagline shines in bright pink letters: "Change the way art is valued." With Patreon, Jack is constructing the future he envisions where "[creators] are going to be paid…and they are going to be valued." When he and Sam didn't find a way to maximize the money earned for their creative pursuits, they built a solution themselves.

Patreon was merely at the start of growing the passion economy and facilitating the Creator Revolution.

Other tools that allow fans to directly pay subscriptions to creators include Ko-Fi, Buy Me a Coffee (and its novel cryptocurrency counterpart, Buy Me a Crypto Coffee), and Twitch during livestreams. More recently, social media giants like Twitter and Tumblr have followed suit with adding further paid subscription and monetization streams for creators (Siberling, 2021). Even though they did not start out as platforms focused on financially supporting creators, they are now consciously aware of the passion economy and are pivoting their focus toward it. YouTube, which has been a creator platform since day one, has expanded its methods for creators to make a living on the platform over the years. In addition to ad revenue, YouTube creators now can also earn money from Premium viewers, sell merchandise, and—just like the subscription platforms and features—sell channel memberships on a monthly basis.

While there is an ever-increasing number of channels for creators to monetize their passions online, they all stem from the same innovation. The ability of social networks to connect every corner of our digital world was critical to the birth of the passion economy. These social platforms provided three key components for creators: a direct channel between creators and consumers, the ability for consumers to discover new creators, and the ability for creators to monetize their goods or services.

"We envision a future in which the value of unique skills and knowledge can be unlocked, augmented, and surfaced to consumers," Li foreshadowed in her essay from 2019.

In the next chapter, we'll see how within the passion economy, influencers are transforming the shopping landscape.

Altogether, we are witnessing a new wave of work. Evolving economic needs and technologies have facilitated the rise of creators and ushered in the passion economy. It is no longer a vision—it is our present *and* our future.

> Creators have ushered in the passion economy, in which creators can now monetize their individuality and hobbies.

The Influencer Takeover

"We have the opportunity to create the future and decide what that's like."

—MAE JEMISON, ASTRONAUT AND AUTHOR

Like other three-year-olds, Ryan Kaji enjoyed playing with toy cars and action figures. No other toddler, however, has turned their love for toys into a multi-million-dollar business like Ryan has.

Ryan is now ten years old, and his YouTube channel "Ryan's World" has over 30 million subscribers and 50 billion views.

He is best known for videos where he unboxes, plays with, and reviews new toys. In his most popular video, Ryan leaps onto a slide in search of giant eggs that contain surprise toys; then, he reveals the toy in each egg and plays with them with unbridled glee. At the end, he waves a giddy farewell to his viewers. The video currently stands at 2 billion views, towering as one of the 60 most-viewed videos on YouTube of all time.

Children all over the world watched his videos for hours every day. In just the month of October in 2016, one year after he launched his channel, Ryan's videos received more than 600 million views. As Jessica Contrera of *The Washington*

Post effectively equated, that's "enough for every minor in the [United States] to have watched him eight times."

Surprisingly, children aren't the only people watching. Companies are also acutely aware of the impact toy reviewing content has on other children. Toymakers and retailers regularly send Ryan toys and merchandise to review. Kids who watch his videos rush to their parents to buy the same toys Ryan has. "If a product gets 10 million, 20 million views, and you see Ryan loves it, or other kids love it, it has a huge impact at retail," said Jim Silver, CEO of the review site Toys, Tots, Pets, and More (Popper, 2016).

From 2018 through 2020, Ryan ended each year as the highest-earning YouTube creator in the world. In that third year, he and his family made nearly 30 million dollars from the channel (Neate, 2020). This figure does not include additional earnings outside his channel's advertisement revenue: according to *Forbes'* Madeline Berg, he has also amassed an estimated 200 million dollars from Ryan-branded products (such as toys and clothing) sold in retail. He has even signed an undisclosed deal with Nickelodeon for his own television series.

Amid the rise of the passion economy, we're entering a never-before-seen era of shopping—one led by creators. And there's no better creator representing it than Ryan.

INFLUENCERS AND SOCIAL COMMERCE

Ryan is one of millions of influencers across social media.

According to the *Merriam-Webster Dictionary*, the word "influencer" was first used in 1662 as a term broadly referring to "a person who inspires or guides the actions of others."

Today, "influencer" has evolved into something more specific. While "influencer" and "creator" are often used interchangeably, there are some nuanced distinctions to be made. In the scope of this book, an **influencer** is anyone who uses social media to grow a following and has the ability to influence their audience's *purchasing* decisions in order to make money. Influencers are a subset of creators, the over-arching category of individuals who consistently create and distribute content to a digital audience.

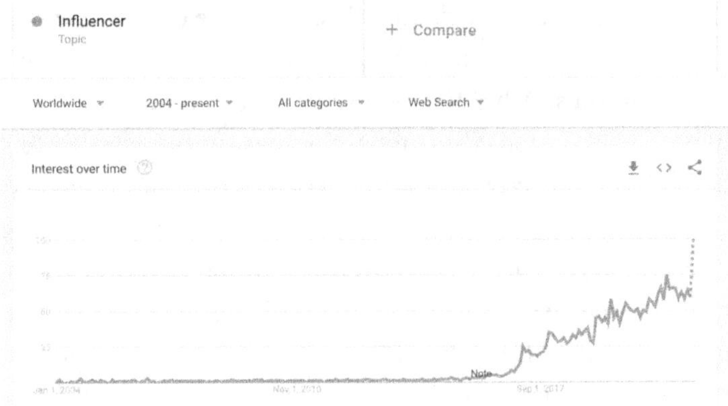

Figure 3.1: As seen on Google Search trends, the interest in influencers as a topic has grown exponentially over time, especially in the last five years. Data source: Google Trends.

The common archetype of an influencer is a woman selling beauty and fashion products via Instagram, but it can go far beyond that: a chef using their Twitter following to promote their line of cookware, a book reviewer promoting books they will receive referral fees from to their TikTok followers, and a streamer telling their Twitch audience to buy their custom merchandise line are all influencers.

With the rise of Instagram, the word "influencer" began to gain traction in 2017 (as seen in Figure 3.1), years after "creator" had already become commonplace in the context of YouTube video producers. Experts and creators themselves find creators are "in it for self-expression," while influencers are "inherently tied to business and monetizing, especially through branded content" (Lorenz, 2019).

The entire landscape of buying and selling is changing as a result of influencers. Consumers have traditionally purchased products from large retail chains and department stores. More recently, **electronic commerce** (also known as e-commerce) has shifted the purchasing process to online shopping sites. Advertisements, which are typically placed in physical locations (bus stops, newspapers, billboards, etc.), television commercials, and online platforms, can influence consumers' purchasing decisions (Google ads, Facebook campaigns, emails, etc.). With the addition of online counterparts to physical stores, commerce has already been gradually moving online. This trend has now been accelerated by the rise and power of influencers, which have ushered in the field of social commerce.

Social commerce is the result of social media colliding with e-commerce. A subset of e-commerce, social commerce involves transactions conducted via any form of online media that offers social interaction.

How social commerce works in practice is influencers can create shoppable videos and images where clicking on custom embedded links (known as affiliate links, which often provide discount codes) opens up a page to the shop where fans can complete the purchase. While some influencers directly sell their own branded merchandise and products to consumers, most of the time they work with third-party brands to facilitate partnerships and create sponsored posts. In exchange for promoting the brand's product, the influencer receives free product samples and either charges direct payments (often split fifty-fifty before and after the content has been published) or earns a percentage of each transaction that is enacted through the affiliate links. For example, in a profile by *Business Insider*, skincare influencer Vi Lai (with a following of around seven hundred thousand) disclosed she earned five thousand dollars per month on average through affiliate links in one year.

In 2020, the US social commerce industry generated nearly 27 billion dollars in retail sales. An August 2021 report from research firm Insider Intelligence projected the industry will be worth nearly 80 billion dollars by the end of 2025, and these figures only point to the US and do not capture the astronomical global impact. In 2020, the global social commerce market was valued at 560 billion dollars—and it doesn't stop there. In fact, this figure is expected to balloon to 2.9 *trillion* dollars by 2026.

Where social commerce outperforms traditional commerce and broader e-commerce is in its ability to speed up sales conversions through a loyal following in an entertaining and relatable manner. Ryan's viewers can vicariously experience his playing experiences and emotions through his content, thereby closing the sales pitch on the toys he is playing with. Better yet, consumers can see physical demonstrations of his toy-playing experiences, allowing viewers to make more informed judgments and evaluations about the toys.

Today, a growing number of people are spending money on social platforms. Almost half (44 percent) of Generation Z has purchased an item online after seeing an influencer recommend it to their audience (Williams, 2020). Incidentally, the keyboard I'm using to write this chapter was purchased after seeing an influencer I follow use the same model.

In particular, TikTok has recently emerged as a product marketing powerhouse—once a product goes viral, it sells out almost immediately. Referred to as the "TikTok made me buy it" phenomenon by *Vox*, the culture of sharing product reviews and recommendations on the platform has caused numerous products to become nearly impossible to buy: a pair of butt-lifting leggings, a cleaning paste called the The Pink Stuff, a Maybelline mascara, three lipsticks that do not leave stains on the insides of face masks, feta cheese, an Eos shaving cream, and countless more. According to *Bloomberg*'s Zheping Huang, China's TikTok counterpart, Douyin, achieved an eye-popping 26 billion dollars in social commerce transactions within the app's first year, soaring beyond TikTok's already transcendent influencer success.

These astounding statistics are in large part due to platforms making it easier to become an influencer (or a creator-turned-influencer). TikTok creator Gerardo Perez (@thegerardoperez) experienced the limitless reach of influencer marketing firsthand when he began publishing videos in late 2019.

As he experimented with video topics and explored TikTok, an app completely foreign to him, Gerardo unlocked a niche TikTok users sought to learn more about: self-help and marketing psychology. His first viral video quickly flashed through five books he recommended every teenager to read, punctuated by his caption, "I wish I would have read these when I was fifteen." TikTok users instantly snatched up the suggested reads and saved the video, propelling the video to over one million views. "I just ordered [one of the books]," one commenter wrote. "[Please] post more recommendations," another added.

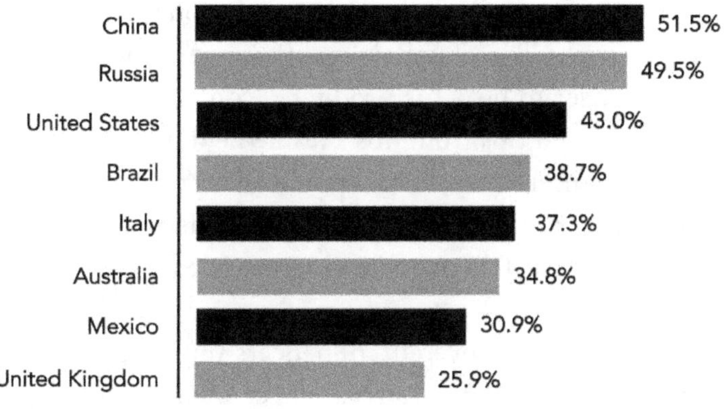

Figure 3.2: Percentage of population of eight selected countries who have purchased at least one product on social media. Data source: Lebow, 2021.

A year later, he published another book recommendation video, this time highlighting Robert Greene's *New York Times* bestselling book, *The 48 Laws of Power.* It instantly captured the eyes of over six million TikTok users and another two million on Instagram. "That video alone caused a sudden spike of over one hundred thousand Google searches of the book within two days after the video was posted. Like…wow," Gerardo recounted to me. Even he could not believe the vast impact he had as an influencer, the bubbly ripples resulting from social media's ease of sharing, growing into monstrous tides.

Realizing the intimate levels of trust he had formed with his audience over time, Gerardo began to leverage his community for monetized brand deals. He partnered with companies such as CXL (a platform of marketing courses) and Headway (an app that offers summaries of popular nonfiction books) to publish sponsored posts that tied in with his content niche and topics.

Two years after he began his creator journey, Gerardo has amassed a TikTok following of over 325 thousand individuals eager to hear his product recommendations and learn firsthand tips from him. While he did not set out to be an influencer, Gerardo has embraced his role and uses his expertise to run Marketing&, an agency dedicated to help brands leverage TikTok through organic content and paid ads.

As Gerardo discovered, influencers impact purchasing decisions on a magnitude ads cannot compare to. A research study conducted by Inmar Intelligence found only three percent of adults surveyed would consider buying a product in-store if it was endorsed by a celebrity (e.g. athlete, actor, musician). In contrast, 60 percent of the American consumers surveyed would buy a product if it were promoted by an influencer through blog reviews or social media posts, according to a study by Collective Bias. This is a staggering 20-times magnitude of difference!

"Influencers are grabbing younger consumers' attention, which is gold dust for so many big companies," Ollie Forsyth, the global community manager at early-stage venture capital firm Antler, told me. "Consumer behaviors are changing, meaning: do we want to spend time [browsing products] online, or do we want to connect with creators who we love so much we just want to spend even more time with them?"

By creating content over time, influencers build credibility and audience loyalty. With the impression you know and trust an influencer, that you have vested interest in them, fans are naturally drawn to believe in their purchasing recommendations as well. This stands in contrast to physical or online advertising, where the individual(s) and messaging in ads are crafted to be generic and distant. Authenticity is a huge factor when it comes to trusting any product review, so consumers lean more toward trusting influencers and their stories, reviews, and demos. Unlike traditional advertisements, selling a product is not the explicit goal of influencers. Instead, we first connect with an influencer as another human being whose background or knowledge we are interested in, and whose values we may share at more depth than a distant celebrity, so it's more similar to trusting a peer's product recommendation than following an advertisement.

In 2020 alone, it's estimated corporate brands spent nearly ten billion dollars on influencer marketing (Drumm, 2021). Influencers have radically altered the landscape of shopping to the point where any consumer or seller who fails to recognize this phenomenon will be left behind.

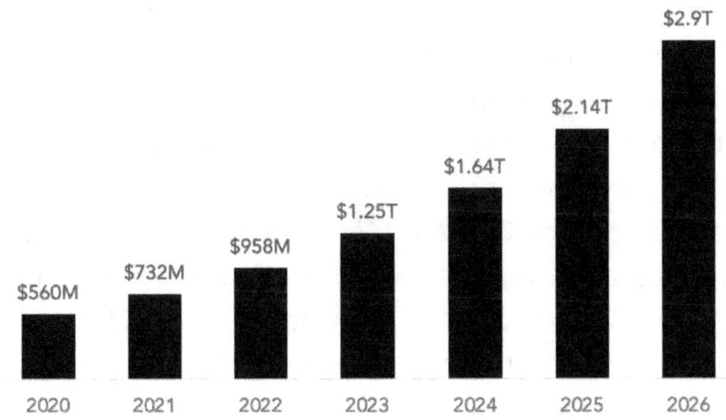

Figure 3.3: 2020–2026 global social commerce market growth and projections (in USD). Data source: Global Industry Analysts, 2021.

DAWN OF LIVE COMMERCE

Born in a rural village in the Yunan province of China, Guowei Jin made ends meet by working as an English teacher during the day and as a pomegranate vendor at night. He never imagined he would become an internet sensation, a Douyin influencer known as "Brother Pomegranate" with a fan base of over seven million. In just the year of 2020, he made 300 million RMB (46 million USD) in fruit sales from livestreaming. Once, he sold 6 million RMB (just under 1 million USD) worth of pomegranates in 20 minutes.

"In the villages, even the most routine moments are fodder for interesting visual content. That's what city people don't have and what they want to see," he told *Bloomberg*'s Selina Xu. While we might think influencers are powerful because of their relatability, here it was Guowei's unique background as a farmer that garnered so much interest and popularity.

Brother Pomegranate is just one of many rural-farmer-turned-influencers. Chengcheng Guo has 2.5 million followers on Douyin, where she livestreams from her family fields to showcase her crops, while fans can instantly tap a link to purchase her produce. In one stream, she squatted down in front of a farm full of vegetables as she beamed into her phone camera, mounted on a phone stand in front of her. In another, she sat down with a plate piled high with mountain fruits, slicing them open to show how ripe and juicy they were to the camera. She takes as many as fifty thousand orders per livestream, which accumulates to over 9 million RMB (1.4 million USD) a month. In the Bắc Giang province of Vietnam, two farmers attracted thirty thousand Facebook Live viewers to their lychee farm and successfully sold eight tons of lychees in a single stint (Dat, 2021).

This trend is not limited to rural farmers either. Dubbed the "King of Lipstick," beauty influencer Jiaqi Li has over fifty million followers on Douyin. On Taobao Live, China's largest livestreaming platform, he once sold over fifteen thousand lipsticks within five minutes (Huang, 2020). These influencers are engaging in a growing sector of social commerce called **live commerce**. Consumers watch livestreamers to discover new products, watch live product demos, and purchase the product without even leaving the broadcast stream.

While live commerce has been around for a few years, its rapid growth was accelerated by the COVID-19 pandemic, which forced the closure of many stores and disrupted supply chains. This left consumers panicking to find products they needed to purchase, and rural farmers were especially hard hit without the regular sales.

Even as the world began to recover from COVID-19 lockdowns, live commerce proved it was here to stay. A 2021 report from McKinsey & Company revealed two-thirds of Chinese consumers have purchased products based on livestreaming influencers' recommendations. Two years ago, the live commerce industry across the nation drove 961 billion RMB (136 billion USD) in annual revenue (Yu, 2020). This figure is expected to rise further—Chinese live commerce sales are expected to reach 423 billion USD by the end of 2022, more than *tripling* the revenue generated just two years prior.

Livestreamers themselves have recognized the importance of their work as well. Zhifang Wu, a Taobao Live influencer who goes by Wei Wei on stream, told the *MIT Technology Review* she "realized live-streaming has greater meaning. It can actually open up entirely new industries and drive local development." As an industry itself, live commerce has been so explosive in China the country's Ministry of Human Resources and Social Security has already listed livestreaming salesperson as a potential career path for people to consider (Shen, 2020).

While live commerce is still in its early stages and is currently concentrated in East and Southeast Asia, it has already demonstrated it is further transforming social commerce and, more broadly, e-commerce. In the United States, numerous live video shopping apps like Talk Shop Live and Ntwrk have emerged; according to *Fast Company*, the industry is expected to hit 35 billion dollars in national sales by 2024. The aforementioned McKinsey & Company report predicts live commerce-initiated sales, despite appearing to be a very niche method of selling products, will account for as much as 10 to 20 percent of all e-commerce by 2026.

Live commerce enhances the benefits of social commerce. Due to the engaging nature of livestreams, it continues to accelerate conversion in a more immersive manner. Two-way conversations are *actual* conversations, spoken aloud on livestreams in response to incoming questions that were asked seconds before. Live demonstrations add to brand appeal and product differentiation, showcasing the versatility and functionalities of every product in a genuine depiction. It amplifies the desire to shop at every turn.

"While the shopping habits of different cultures may differ, younger consumers, regardless of where they live, are similar in how they use social media to connect," said Alessandro Bogliari, co-founder and CEO of The Influencer Marketing Factory, in a feature by *Retail Dive*. "Livestreaming taps into that trait because, unlike the shopping channel model, it gives viewers the ability to have a two-way conversation with the host." With younger generations growing up as digital natives and fully embracing social media, they all use their phones and are eager to tune in to livestreams of their favorite influencers, even when they may not be seeking to buy anything in particular.

In this chapter, we explored another Societal Shift: social commerce, including the new phenomenon of live commerce, is transforming the future of shopping. Whether you are looking to buy pomegranates, makeup, or toys, you will inevitably come across the recommendations of influencers. In Chapter 4, we will see how the impact of creators has expanded beyond economic effects to punctuate their presence as educators as well.

> An influencer is a type of creator who uses social media to influence their audience's purchasing decisions. Influencers have revolutionized how products are bought and sold through social commerce and live commerce.

CHAPTER 4

The Education Transformation

*"The beautiful thing about learning is
no one can take it away from you."*

—B.B. KING, MUSICIAN, SONGWRITER, AND PRODUCER

Since 2009, Claudine James has been teaching English to generations of middle school students. While most middle school teachers instruct classes of 20 to 30 students at a time, Claudine currently teaches daily to a worldwide following of over 3 million on TikTok under the handle @ iamthatenglishteacher.

When the COVID-19 pandemic struck and all education turned virtual, Claudine began recording her grammar lessons for her students to watch. However, she noticed the number of views on her videos was consistently lower than her class size. "I have twenty-two students, but my videos only have seven views. You know something's wrong," Claudine said to me with a laugh.

Her students suggested she post her videos on TikTok, where they believed they would be better able to engage with the lessons. They simply did not want to watch one long lecture video after another.

Claudine, despite being fifty-four years old and not exactly the TikTok demographic you might expect, followed her students' advice. After receiving a quick crash course from her students and goddaughter on how the social network app worked, she posted her first TikTok video on November 30, 2020. Standing in front of a whiteboard, she taught capitalization rules for nouns in a short, snappy manner. All in all, the video lesson lasted only 47 seconds. Claudine then went to bed without giving the video much thought.

When she woke up the next morning, she discovered she had gained one thousand followers overnight.

Claudine spent that weekend posting more videos and answering grammar questions TikTok users posted in response. By the time she returned to school on Monday, she already had over 10,000 followers. When I spoke with her nine months later, Claudine had an audience of 2.6 million followers from over 80 countries, and she has only grown more since then.

As a long-time teacher, Claudine wasn't new to receiving recognition for her instruction. She holds numerous teaching certifications and has received countless awards for her classroom education. But for the first time, she had a seal of approval on her instruction from her own students; rather than feeling forced to be in her classroom, they now voluntarily chose to engage with her educational videos on their favorite platform. Furthermore, when Claudine's students watched her videos, they saw so many other people who were eager to learn from her, which inspired them to be more involved in their lessons.

The transition from educator to creator felt natural to her. "It was such an easy transition, I never felt a bump," Claudine said. Posting her videos on TikTok was still teaching, albeit now to a larger audience.

According to *Forbes*, Generation Z and Millennials have average attention spans of eight seconds and twelve seconds, respectively. In a time when attention is so precious to capture, they are carefully choosing what to devote their attention to—and for many, the people they choose to listen to the most are creators. Creators like Claudine create engaging content the rest of us can pick and choose based on what is the most interesting, tailored, and relevant to us. Not only were Claudine's students and followers more engaged and informed, but as the creator, she discovered a new way to enjoy and share the process of teaching. It turned out to be a win-win situation for all parties.

Traditional education has long centered around physical institutions and resources like books and encyclopedias. The advent of the internet brought about search engines and, more recently, online courses. However, the majority of education continues to take place in the classroom: a teacher delivers knowledge to students in a school setting over long blocks of time, and that knowledge is reinforced through follow-up discussions, assignments, and exams.

The Creator Revolution has resulted in a new mode of education: education obtained directly from creators. Specifically, this wave is being ushered in by a group of creators who I refer to as **knowledge creators**, content creators who focus on sharing information about specific niches. They offer value in the form of knowledge (as broadly as that may be defined) and publish content centered around it. There are no exams or essays, just direct interaction with creators.

Many students in the past fifteen years have grown up reading, watching, and consuming content to supplement their learning in school. Khan Academy's founder, Sal Khan, started posting math videos on YouTube in 2006; today, over fifteen million individuals around the world learn on Khan Academy every month. John and Hank Green launched the Crash Course YouTube channel in 2011 to provide free educational videos on a range of subjects, including world history and biology; since then, their videos have been viewed over 1.6 billion times and shared by educators around the globe. Science storyteller duo ASAPScience (1.7 billion views since 2012), advanced mathematics educator 3Blue1Brown (250 million views since 2015), and kindergarten literacy and numeracy channel Akili and Me (370 million views since 2016) are several more examples of stellar creators whose content has been pivotal in complementing students' educational journeys.

But the scope of knowledge creators isn't just limited to traditional school subjects like math or writing. It also includes common life skills that aren't usually taught in school—makeup, finances, and cooking, to name a few. A 2021 survey by *The Ascent* found 91 percent of Gen Z investors and 75 percent of millennial investors obtain their investing knowledge through social media. Searching "food hacks" on Google yields a staggering 42 million videos on cooking tricks and techniques, with the top video "Ultimate Food Hacks Compilation" by how-to lifestyle YouTube channel DaveHax garnering over 24 million views alone.

Knowledge creators are ushering in a new wave of education that aims to democratize access to information in a social manner. Consequently, when any individual can publish and share content online, the rate at which knowledge can be shared will increase exponentially over time.

In this chapter, we will examine what knowledge creators can bring to augment education, which I will define broadly as any form of instruction that seeks to inform. Sometimes this type of content goes one step further, encouraging learners to engage with and advocate for important causes. However, due to the risks and consequences of disseminating misinformation, a future of learning completely led by creators may not be ideal either. Ultimately, it is up to us to decide what role knowledge creators will play in shaping the education of current and future generations.

KNOWLEDGE CREATORS

Rajya Atluri was a graduating senior in college who hopped onto TikTok for fun. She posted videos about her hobbies and life interests, one of which was makeup. Standing in front of her camera, Rajya would apply makeup while narrating her process and describing her products. In one video, she demonstrated a color correction method that worked well for her darker skin tone, using a merely five-dollar concealer to do so. That video resonated with many viewers and went viral, later being featured in *Allure* magazine as one of the best makeup tutorials ever to be published on TikTok. Most other makeup videos and tutorials used expensive products that only worked for a few skin tones. Her audience loved being able to finally find easily accessible products that fit their darker skin tones.

As she posted more videos about makeup and skincare, she realized being a content creator enabled her to reach a large number of people who she would not have been able to reach otherwise. Now a part-time creator with over one million likes on TikTok (@rajyaatluri), Rajya educates people on wellness, beauty tips, and products many individuals would not have known about otherwise. She is an influencer, but she considers herself a knowledge creator first and foremost.

"Creators are offering a whole new type of education different from what we've been seeing," she shared in our conversation. "I think that has a lot of potential because it's like a whole new avenue of learning."

The type of education knowledge creators offer is unique in that it can be customized to each individual. This stands in stark contrast with the traditional one-size-fits-all, large lecture room style school instruction most of us are accustomed to. Rajya has discovered this has been extremely helpful for individuals seeking beauty insights: "Followers can ask their favorite creators questions and get customized advice or feedback. That is really useful for something like beauty, where your skin, face, and everything else are unique."

Furthermore, the large and growing number of creators allows for an expansive range of content online. This can address more needs and questions people have about their experiences and knowledge, which vary from individual to individual. Rajya is not the only wellness and skincare creator on the internet. Because of the ease with which content can be published online, others with different skin tones can offer their insights on the best methods, resources, and products for their respective skin tones, as Rajya has done. The ability to customize and tailor one's education is a unique advantage that is extremely challenging to replicate in a traditional classroom setting.

Ollie Forsyth, the global community manager at early-stage venture capital firm Antler who we met in Chapter 3, is excited about the role creators will play in the future of education. "Creators are becoming the new high school teachers," he remarked during our interview.

In addition to informing the public about traditional school topics and lifestyle advice, creator-educators can take on the role of activists as well. The Creator Revolution has given rise to individuals like Macy Lee, a Filipina mental health activist whose content has reached over eight hundred thousand individuals worldwide.

Macy began her advocacy work at the age of fourteen, when she launched a blog sharing personal mental health stories about herself and her family members. She wished to normalize the conversation about mental health struggles and experiences. The more she wrote, the more she discovered her readers were eager to learn about mental health issues, which were rarely discussed in school. So, Macy sought to start conversations about them through her content.

Today, she has expanded her content formats to webinars, Instagram infographics, videos, livestreams, and a podcast, all of which aim to educate and discuss topics across the spectrum of mental health, such as depression, post-traumatic stress disorder, and intersectionality. "I use social media not just for myself," Macy firmly stated to me. She considers herself an activist foremost, where she primarily uses her "platform for advocacy."

Echoing Macy's perspective, Pranjal Jain sees content as a mechanism to "raise awareness, share what [she's] up to, and create conversation." As the co-founder of Global Girlhood, a nonprofit organization revolutionizing the empowerment of women around the globe, and the co-host of the podcast *Brown Sugar*, she uses content creation to elevate her advocacy and education work.

"I like the idea social media lets me share whatever it is that I'm thinking," Pranjal told me while discussing her thoughts on content platforms, "because you never know who might be listening and who might be feeling like they're heard, or who might be able to share more and teach me." For her, education traverses in both directions in the world of content: she shares and educates her audience as a creator, and she learns from other creators and her own audience as well.

Her podcast centers on feminism, sexuality, and dating—all of which are taboo topics in many cultures, including the South Asian community, the podcast's target audience. When Pranjal spoke with her friend, both of them felt they had to go out of their way to seek knowledge and learn about these topics, thereby "accumulating a treasure chest of stories and information" that would be helpful to others just like them. They recognized the importance of speaking up and breaking the stigma, and thus decided to launch this endeavor.

A podcast, like any other form of content, is not an easy project to launch. For each episode, the duo needed to brainstorm topics, write the episode, edit the script, plan and invite guests, create a marketing strategy, record the episode, and edit the audio before they could finally publish it. But they understood how the podcast allowed their audience and community to find and access information that was not readily available to them, knowledge they would have liked to have known sooner.

As creators, Macy and Pranjal can now reach an audience of a much larger scale in order to advocate for and educate the public on important issues. Content creation provides activists with an instantaneous magnified audience to teach to, right beneath their fingertips.

The creators in this chapter have all recognized the immense power digital content has in democratizing access to education and knowledge, no matter what genre the knowledge falls under. Altogether, knowledge creators offer a new form of education that has three advantages over traditional classroom education: it can be customizable, engaging, and scalable.

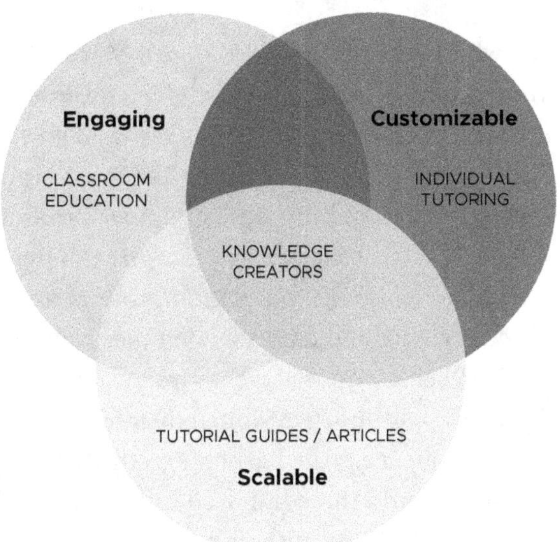

Figure 4.1: How knowledge creators fit at the intersection of offering engaging, scalable, and customizable education.

MISINFORMATION

While knowledge creators offer great advantages, they are far from perfect. **Misinformation**, whether spread intentionally or not, jeopardizes the credibility of their contributions.

The ease of creating content comes with a caveat: not all information on the internet is vetted. Unlike traditional journalism, where editors perform diligent fact-checking, there is no easy way to validate every piece of content found on the internet. As a result, misinformation can spread rapidly and rampantly.

Earlier in the chapter, we learned about how Rajya educates her followers on skincare products and wellness resources. There are thousands of other beauty influencers like her, all of whom conduct varying degrees of research and validation prior to publishing content. Tiara Willis, an esthetician who heads the Twitter account @MakeupForWOC (with over 285,000 followers), bemoans the misinformation creators spread in an attempt to gain views and go viral.

"It's a lot of experiments and DIYs, like 'I put pineapples on my face and it cleared my skin, and now a million people are trying it,'" she told *Vox* in 2021. For example, viral TikToks peddled a brand's foundation product until more users started trying it and realized it left them with creased, oily faces. One beauty tip that went viral on TikTok recommended people apply bleach to whiten their teeth, which had far worse consequences. The hashtag "teethwhitening" has since amassed around three hundred million views on the platform, and the majority of these posts are associated with this trend, even though administering bleach to whiten teeth can cause "permanent damage" (Criddle, 2020).

A knowledge creator may disseminate information that is appropriate for themselves but not for others. Makeup products, in particular, are not universal—such as for people of different skin complexions—but product reviews tend to lack nuance and consideration of all audiences.

Furthermore, it is often difficult to differentiate an authentic product demonstration from a sponsored advertisement. With over 50,000 followers across TikTok and Instagram, Tanupa (@tanupaskincare) has published videos giving honest reviews of skincare and beauty products for two years. When she partners with brands to do sponsored collaborations, she always requests two weeks of product testing before she commits to the partnership to ensure its quality. However, this is not the case for all influencers. Tanupa, now an experienced creator, realized over time many videos are not what they appear to be. "Someone can say 'this completely transformed my skin!' when they are being paid to do so," she explained to me, "and it's a very frustrating thing, but I think more of my frustration has to do with brands."

Many countries have laws prohibiting deceptive advertising. In the United States, for example, the Federal Trade Commission enacted legislation stating, "Under the law, claims in advertisements must be truthful, cannot be deceptive or unfair, and must be evidence-based." As a result, influencers must use prominent and simple language, such as "#ad" or "Thanks to [brand] for sponsoring me," at the beginning of captions of sponsored posts and videos. This allows fans to understand right away the post is an advertisement rather than an authentic recommendation.

Behind the scenes, however, some brands go to great lengths to skirt around these regulations in the name of promoting authenticity. Tanupa revealed she has heard of some brands instructing influencers to not use hashtags like "#sponsored," to place such language as far in the back of the caption as possible to hide them, or to avoid the language entirely—all in order to make the content appear as organic as possible. This not only takes advantage of naive, especially novice, influencers who are unaware these are illegal practices to engage in, but it also misleads fans into believing these are genuine recommendations made by their trusted creator.

The danger of purchasing products based on the hype built by strangers on the internet is they may not be vetted accurately or be helpful to all audiences. But when these pieces of content deal with topics teetering the line of life and death, human lives are put in jeopardy. Dr. Vicki Chan, an ophthalmologist, was one of the first to recognize this. A long-time user of social media, Vicki (@vickichanmd) primarily sought to use content to humanize the field of medicine, sharing her journey as both a doctor and a mom.

But when the COVID-19 pandemic struck, she witnessed medical misinformation spiraling out of control all over social media. Videos created by individuals with no professional medical background went viral, drowning out the opinions of doctors and medical experts in news sources.

"There's very little accountability for creators. People can say whatever they want to say on social media," Vicki said over a video call. In contrast, spreading misinformation can cost physicians their medical license (Hiltzik, 2021). Vicki further explained, "Creators have no licenses and nearly nothing to lose. If they get in trouble, at most their account gets shut down, right? And then they go somewhere else, to another platform."

Seeing the imminent issue at hand, Vicki decided to use her knowledge as a medical professional to confront it head on. She published videos and online resources debunking COVID-19 myths and explaining concepts like immunity, antibodies, and vaccines in layman's terms. Given her specialty in eye and vision care as an ophthalmologist, Vicki also shared knowledge about eye disorders and treatments that were not widely known. With over 450,000 followers across TikTok and Instagram today, she has grown a global audience who wants to learn accurate health-related information from a medical professional.

Despite the impact she has created, Vicki recognizes misinformation cannot be solved by one creator or one physician alone: "I think doctors, more and more, are realizing we have to fight [medical] misinformation ourselves—because if we don't do this, then who else is going to?" It helps that content creation is far more scalable than private doctor appointments. In her office, Vicki can only advise one person at a time, which can get exhausting and repetitive very quickly.

She has reached millions at once through her videos, and with that power, she hopes accurate, professionally-vetted information will eventually squash out the inaccurate counterpart.

Because of the power and reach knowledge creators have, creators who specialize in spreading misinformation have emerged as an industry. They promote controversial—and sometimes downright dangerous—policies and ideologies. While they are still technically teaching and advocating, what they are advocating for may endanger many.

In 2021, *Vice* discovered an unknown agency had hired verified, high-profile Twitter users in Kenya to actively participate in structured harassment and disinformation campaigns targeting activists and members of the country's judiciary. For up to fifteen dollars a day, these creators—"disinformation influencers," as the publication dubbed them—preached unfounded claims and propaganda statements under preplanned hashtags. By seeing verified users proclaim these opinions, a Twitter user would be more prone to believe them. The campaign's goal was simple: sway public opinion and undermine citizens' trust in Kenya's judiciary.

"The biggest threat is that it pollutes the information ecosystem to an extent that it becomes so difficult for the citizens to separate the facts from the falsehoods," said Alphonce Shiundu, the Kenya editor of Africa Check. "When a disinformation campaign is carried out, there's usually cross-pollination of the disinformation, say a screenshot from Twitter being shared on Facebook, WhatsApp, and Instagram and such, and then it jumps off those platforms into the word-of-mouth grapevines, and before you know it, it is being repeated as fact in marketplaces."

According to a 2020 report published by the University of Oxford, the disinformation-for-hire industry is estimated to have earned nearly 60 million dollars from campaigns that have hired these firms since 2009. This is a frightening figure that will only continue to grow until a good solution is found.

It is exciting that the Creator Revolution has paved a new avenue of education in knowledge creators. They are able to offer instruction in engaging and customizable formats, and the wide reach of online content means it is so much easier to democratize access to knowledge from all pockets of information. However, entrusting education to knowledge creators and placing this role in their hands comes at the present risk of disseminating misinformation. This issue is not a one-sided effort, nor can it be solved quickly. It is a problem that needs to be jointly solved by creators, consumers, social platforms, and society as a whole.

> Knowledge creators offer a new type of education that is customizable, engaging, and scalable. However, education from knowledge creators carries the risk of misinformation.

CHAPTER 5

The Media Makeover

*"If you want to be the star, create the show.
Don't wait. Make your own opportunities.
There's no better time than to start today."*

—ANNA AKANA, FILMMAKER, ACTRESS,

AND YOUTUBE CREATOR

Back in 2007, Issa Rae was a college student writing school plays and uploading videos onto YouTube and Facebook for fun. Fifteen years later, she has become a household name as the writer, producer, and starring actress of the award-winning television series *Insecure*.

At Stanford, she was an active member of the campus's theater community. In a 2012 profile, the *Stanford Magazine* recalled how Issa, née Jo-Issa Rae Diop, "staged adaptations of Spike Lee movies and a Motown version of *Grease* and filmed *Dorm Diaries*, a gossipy mockumentary." To this day, "prospective students still check out the series for a peek at Black life at Stanford." Following the positive reception to *Dorm Diaries*, she continued to pursue her love for writing and filmmaking.

However, the more she observed existing films, the more she had become disillusioned with the tokenization of Black women in traditional media. In her memoir *The Misadventures of Awkward Black Girl*, she remembered questioning, "How hard is it to portray a three-dimensional woman of color on television or in film?"

Issa sought to change that—by creating her own content that demonstrated otherwise.

In 2011, she published a new comedy series *Awkward Black Girl* on YouTube. The series, written by and starring herself, followed the life of a woman navigating embarrassing situations of romance, friendship, and office politics as an awkward twenty-something introvert. It was an instant viral hit, quickly racking up millions of views through word-of-mouth spread, social media, and mainstream news coverage. The series portrayed Black women as multi-faceted, diverse characters, which was a breath of fresh air that resonated with many viewers. When funds started to run out, Issa used Kickstarter, an online crowdfunding platform, and Patreon, the subscription-driven creator membership tool we learned about in Chapter 2, to keep the series afloat.

As her content received more widespread attention, her brand and reputation as a filmmaker and screenwriter soared. While Hollywood powerbrokers had previously rejected Issa's pitches years ago, telling her no market existed for the stories she wanted to tell, the undeniable success and metrics of her content had now caught the attention of studios and television producers (Giorgis, 2021). It paved the path for her to write and star in *Insecure*, which received eleven Emmy nominations in its five-season run. Furthermore, it was well-heralded for its authentic storytelling; at the 2017 Peabody Awards, the show was honored for "creating a series that authentically captures the lives of everyday young Black people in modern society."

WarnerMedia, HBO's parent company, announced a five-year contract extension with her for future film and television productions in 2021. Without YouTube, Kickstarter, Patreon, and the power of the Creator Revolution, Issa could not have as easily propelled her talent, visions, and stories to mainstream media.

In Chapter 4, we looked at how the Creator Revolution has given birth to a new education model while also introducing the risk of misinformation. With these considerations in mind, in this chapter we will add to these discussions by examining how creators have also transformed the media landscape, particularly in the realms of fictional entertainment and news journalism.

REIMAGINED FICTIONAL ENTERTAINMENT

Elle Griffin had always considered herself a writer. She launched a food blog in college and a health blog when she started her first job, before eventually making a full career pivot into the journalism industry. But like many writers, she wanted to go further. Elle wanted to publish a novel.

She sat down and spent a few months at home writing her book, a gothic novel written in the vein of *Dracula*, *The Phantom of the Opera*, and *The Count of Monte Cristo*. In line with the publishing process of fiction books, she began to pitch her manuscript to agents.

However, as she researched the publishing industry in greater depth, she realized she wanted something different. Even with the most well-established agents and publishers, her best-case scenario appeared to be around five thousand book sales. That was already a big assumption to make; in 2021, *The New York Times* revealed "98 percent of the books that publishers released in 2020 sold fewer than five thousand copies." But then the publisher would take away an estimated 75 percent of her profits and retain her intellectual property rights for the next decade.

"[I realized] I had to take matters into my own hands," she reflected in our conversation. "I'm tying myself into this contract where there's nothing I can do to further my books. So I just said, 'Okay, I'm going to start marketing it myself.'"

Thus, Elle decided to publish her novel in a different method: as a serial. A serial is a format where a single larger work is published in smaller installments. She releases one chapter a week on Substack, which is dominated by nonfiction and professionals-targeted newsletters, until her book is completed. The first few chapters are free, and after that she begins to charge five dollars per month. Under this model, Elle reasoned, if she could reach one hundred paid readers, she'd be guaranteed five hundred dollars per month from her book.

Serials, particularly **serialized fiction** works, are not a new concept. Charles Dickens famously published his novels through installments in literary magazines. Harriet Beecher Stowe's *Uncle Tom's Cabin* was published over a forty-week period in a newspaper. Numerous other famous classics, including Leo Tolstoy's *Anna Karenina*, Sir Arthur Conan Doyle's *The Hound of the Baskervilles*, and Agatha Christie's *And Then There Were None,* were all originally released as serial novels (Schlottman, 2021).

Over time, however, it has become increasingly rare for contemporary fiction authors to serialize their novels. Critics of serialized publishing pointed to the format's limitations, which often resulted in long pieces of text, inconsistent storylines, plot holes that were discovered only when a novel was viewed as a whole, and unnecessary repetition. But serialized fiction has seen a surge in recent years as a new format for creators to better grow their audience and build brand loyalty. When you publish a book, your readers must wait years for your next book, by which time they may have lost interest or forgotten about you. When you release a chapter at a time, your readers wait with bated breath from week to week, month to month, and are actively thinking about your writing throughout the publishing process.

A year into launching her newsletter, which offers her serialized book as well as essays reflecting on her writing experience and relevant publishing resources, Elle revealed she had over 4,000 total newsletter subscribers and 170 paying subscribers, earning 10,000 dollars in revenue. She continues to write her novels and publish her thoughts, and she hopes to be able to write her newsletter fulltime by the end of 2023.

Elle is just one of many writers who have taken advantage of the shifting landscape of written media. As a writer who started in the fanfiction world, I published one chapter a week on a set day, so my readers knew when to expect the new chapter every week, on platforms like Archive of Our Own, Wattpad, Royal Road, and Fanfiction.net. Other online fiction hubs like LiveJournal, Webnovel, Inkitt, and Kindle Vella further broaden the scope of serialized fiction platforms.

Wattpad, in particular, carries nearly one billion stories. Not only is it a popular site for discovering and reading fiction, with over ninety million users roaming its shelves of stories every month, Wattpad has also become a successful springboard for big screen hits. Netflix film franchise *The Kissing Booth* was adapted from a Wattpad novel that was eventually picked up and published by Penguin Random House; the romantic drama film *After* originated from a One Direction fanfiction written by Anna Todd and released on Wattpad, which was then adapted into a *New York Times* bestselling book published by Simon & Schuster. While I was writing this book, ViacomCBS announced a new partnership with Wattpad to create more original series adapting stories from the site (Errens, 2021).

China has taken this trend to a new level. In 2021, *China Daily* reported half of the country's netizens (about 455 million people) have developed a regular habit of reading serialized novels online, on platforms such as Qidian and Jinjiangwenxuecheng. According to *Tencent News*, these sites have built a massive 28.8 billion RMB (4.5 billion USD) web literature industry. As tracked by Guduo data, a whopping 34 of the top 50 most watched Chinese television series (on TV and streaming services) were adapted from serialized web novels.

So not only has the Creator Revolution allowed writers like Elle and me to capitalize on our community to distribute their fictional stories, online content is feeding into the traditional media pipeline to showcase stories and voices anyone on the internet can create.

It's worth noting this trend is not limited to written content. At the beginning of this chapter, we saw how YouTube served as a launchpad for Issa Rae to land her own productions to write and star in. Now-defunct six-second video clip app Vine launched the acting career of Liza Koshy, who starred in Hulu's *Freakish* and Netflix's *Work It* (Kroll, 2020). Ariel Martin, known by her online alias Baby Ariel, was an early creator on TikTok's predecessor musical.ly before starring in a Disney Channel original movie (Valentine, 2020). Casting agents must now scour video platforms on a regular basis to find fresh faces and talent, which is no longer a luxury but a necessity.

There is no denying big-screen studio productions and streaming services are still important mediums for enjoying fictional entertainment today. But the sources of talent and ideas increasingly stem from the creator ecosystem, and we must not overlook the Creator Revolution's impact on moving the industry forward.

DECENTRALIZED NEWS JOURNALISM

Casey Newton had been a journalist for over eighteen years, seven of which he spent reporting for *The Verge*. His pieces have been nominated for National Magazine Awards. Despite that, he decided to leave the world of traditional journalism to launch his own newsletter.

During his time at *The Verge*, he published over 570 issues of *The Interface* newsletter to more than twenty thousand subscribers. The newsletter discussed technology, social media, and issues around disinformation and content moderation. While he couldn't keep the newsletter after he departed the publication, he had amassed a sizable audience who followed him to Substack, where he started his own email newsletter, *Platformer*, in 2020.

Many journalists have opted to become independent creators on open publishing platforms like Substack, Ghost, Medium, and Mirror due to the steady decline of traditional news journalism. A recent study conducted by the University of North Carolina revealed more than 25 percent of newspapers in the United States have died in the last fifteen years, and roughly half of all newspaper jobs were eliminated in that timespan (Abernathy, 2020).

Casey himself has observed these changes in his nearly two decades of being a journalist. "The entire time, I've been nervous about what's going on in the ad market. First I saw the web come along and disrupt the print newspapers I was working for. Then the platforms came along and disrupted the digital properties I was working for. Along the way, thousands of really talented journalists lost their jobs," he reflected earnestly in an interview with *OneZero* in 2020.

Casey didn't want to become another statistic. By being a creator, he could control his own narrative and outcome. Unlike traditional news journalism, which requires a reader to follow a publication, this new model allows you to follow individual journalists or creators.

"You might follow a publication, but it's more likely you care about an individual reporter or writer or YouTuber or podcaster," Casey said to *The New York Times*'s Marc Tracy. "People are increasingly willing to pay to support those people."

Substack's reliance on email distribution, rather than social media or search engines, promoted a one-on-one relationship between writers and readers that both sides value. There are also limits to how much traditional media companies could pay journalists, whereas Casey felt he had "uncapped upside" as an independent creator (Jeong, 2020). According to the salary comparison website Payscale, the average base salary for a journalist is around 42,000 dollars, up to 80,000 dollars on the higher end. In comparison, for a newsletter writer to earn 100,000 dollars a year, one only needs 1,667 readers to subscribe for five dollars every month.

"It's not easy—it takes time, dedication, and care—but it's more doable than ever," Substack co-founder Hamish McKenzie wrote in his own newsletter. While Substack certainly does not have the viewership cable television channels (e.g. MSNBC, Fox News, CNN) and popular digital news publications (e.g. *The New York Times, The Washington Post*) do, the trend of growth shows readers increasingly want to follow specific creators more than news media organizations. According to traffic analysis platform SimilarWeb, Substack saw an 80 percent increase in readership in 2021. In contrast, the five aforementioned channels and publications saw a significant drop (decline rates of -25 to -44 percent) of traffic during the same timeframe (Bauder, 2021).

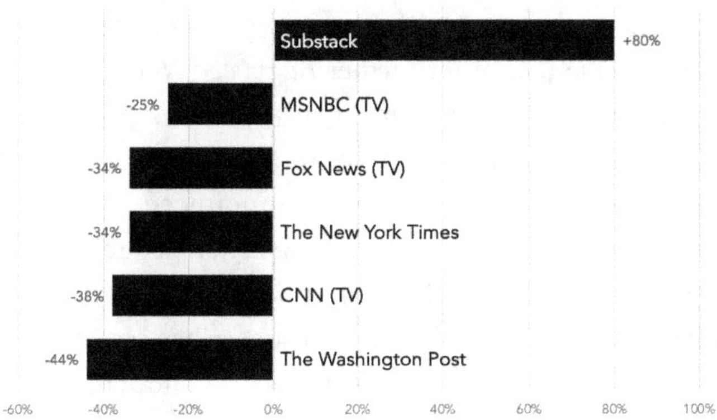

Figure 5.1: Comparison of traffic in 2021 across different news media (television and digital journalism). Data sources: Bauder, 2021 and SimilarWeb, 2021.

Building a robust, close-knit community was another challenge when tied to large media organizations. After going independent, Casey launched a Discord server to accompany his newsletter. This was an advancement new to journalists but familiar to creators, and it proved to be extremely effective for his newsletter's growth. This addition provided a setting for readers to meet others interested in relevant topics, discuss current events, and pitch topics for Casey to write about.

Casey is not the only journalist who has left their news organizations to pursue their own independent endeavors. Emily Atkin, a former climate staff writer at *The New Republic* magazine, announced her new daily climate crisis newsletter *HEATED* on Twitter in September of 2019, a full year before Casey had made his move. After spending five years at *BuzzFeed News* as a senior technology reporter, Alex Kantrowitz announced his departure to launch his own newsletter and podcast, *Big Technology*, in mid-2020. Anne Helen Petersen, another former *BuzzFeed News* journalist, turned her sporadic, "Sunday treat"-like newsletter *Culture Study* into her fulltime job three months later.

In the same year, Matt Taibbi announced his fulltime transition to writing his personal newsletter on Substack after seventeen years writing for *Rolling Stone*. "I believe the path for independent journalists is in a subscriber-based model," he wrote in his first newsletter piece. "Compensation in news media traditionally involves a reporter working for a corporation or a wealthy patron, who ostensibly paid staff with revenue from advertising and subscriptions. This used to be necessary because delivering content was expensive and required additional labor: design, printing, distribution, marketing, etc. Distribution is instant now, design can be automated, and there are no printing costs. The logical endgame is cutting out middle steps and having journalists work directly for readers…This should not only be sustainable, but the preferable way to go."

One year later, in January of 2022, video journalist and producer Cleo Abram departed *Vox* after five years at the company to launch her own show *Huge If True* on YouTube and TikTok. "[O]ver the last 2 years, I've started to feel a shift in the way we as a society cover things I care about…," she wrote on her Twitter. "What can I do, as a journalist, to rigorously engage with new ideas earlier?" Her solution was to start her own endeavor, which would give her more creative freedom and control.

These are just six of the many journalists who have left the world of traditional journalism behind to become independent creators. However, the trending shifts in journalism run deeper than existing reporters becoming creators. We must also consider everyday content consumers and the roles they play in news distribution and consumption, such as digital artist Kim Saira.

Kim never thought her design skills would lead to her role as a well-regarded creator who shares news and resources on Instagram (@kimsaira). At the start of 2021, they were frustrated with the lack of news coverage surrounding the then-recent string of violent hate crimes committed against Asian Americans. So, she decided to take on this problem herself, conducting extensive research on the subject and then publishing two infographics about it on Instagram. The two posts went viral, receiving over 460,000 views combined, achieving their goal of raising awareness and sharing effective and relevant resources.

Kim realized that for many Instagram users "the infographics operated as the news," she shared in our interview. Today, over one hundred thousand people follow them on the platform, eager to learn more and curate resources from their infographics.

The media industry has been gradually consolidating over the years. In the United States, this has resulted in only *six* corporations (Comcast, Disney, AT&T, ViacomCBS, Sony, Fox) controlling 90 percent of all media in the country, as documented by *Business Insider*. In a world of media so dominated by a select few, the rise of the Creator Revolution has opened the floodgates toward a more decentralized future of news distribution.

From the emergence of the passion economy to the transformation of e-commerce, a re-imagining of education to a media makeover, Part I of this book, "Societal Shifts," has highlighted several critical areas in which creators are revolutionizing society. In the following section, we will look at how creators revolutionize themselves, beginning with how content opens up previously unimaginable windows of opportunity.

> Creators have transformed the media landscape by decentralizing content, aggregating ideas and talents, and leveraging community-driven resources, as evident in fictional entertainment and news journalism.

PART II:

SELF-MADE SUCCESS

Part II examines how the Creator Revolution has given us a new reality: one in which you can create your own success. In pursuing your passions, you can control your own narrative and outcome.

Chapter 6 demonstrates how being a creator can pave the way for new and unforeseen opportunities.

Chapter 7 highlights the similarities between a creator and an entrepreneur, and points to how creators can use their content to springboard themselves into entrepreneurs.

Chapter 8 builds on Chapter 7 to showcase how creators are the most valuable brands of our future. Not only are creators leading businesses, creators are their own businesses and follow the steps of a typical business development cycle.

Chapter 9 considers the critical role creators play in amplifying representation in media.

CHAPTER 6

Creators as Trailblazers

"It is not in the stars to hold our destiny but in ourselves."

—WILLIAM SHAKESPEARE, PLAYWRIGHT AND POET

Jonathan Javier looked at his email inbox with great dismay. One job rejection after another trickled in, and he was at a loss for what to do.

A first-generation Filipino American student attending a small university, Jonathan found little support for his career search journey. He realized if he wanted to work for the companies he dreamed of, he couldn't just sit back and wait for opportunities to float his way. Instead, he needed to be proactive—whether it was meeting people, building relationships, or learning more about the companies he wanted to join, he needed to try anything to inch one step closer to his dreams.

So, he turned to social media to achieve exactly that, creatively leveraging LinkedIn to build his personal brand beyond its core functionality of showcasing his online resume. "I realized by utilizing LinkedIn, creating a personal brand, and developing content, you could meet with people and gain a lot of insights into the companies you hope to learn more about," he recalled to me. In addition to sending carefully researched and personalized outreach messages to grow his network, Jonathan began to post weekly about events he planned to attend related to his target companies. His posts caught the eye of employees and recruiters there, which assisted in him soon receiving job offers from large technology companies where few students from his school had previously worked.

As *Forbes*'s Dana Brownlee skillfully observed, Jonathan's "smartest move was deciding to stop trying to win a game stacked against him from the start and instead find a way to reinvent it."

Jonathan's online content also attracted an unexpected collaborator, Jerry Lee. A Korean American immigrant, Jerry also understood the agony of the job search process firsthand. After connecting on LinkedIn and talking more in-depth, Jonathan and Jerry realized they shared a strong desire to help others from humble beginnings like their own to achieve career success. The pair began hosting free university workshops about the career search and recruiting process and publicized the events on LinkedIn. When comments and requests for more events poured in, they realized the magnitude of the problem far exceeded their expectations.

"We saw a need for people, especially those who came from underprivileged, underrepresented backgrounds, who didn't have the necessary knowledge for their job search. We wanted to fulfill this need and help bridge that information gap," Jonathan said. "So we asked ourselves, 'How do we start something to help people?'"

The duo scaled their efforts from in-person workshops into career consulting firm Wonsulting, using social media platforms like LinkedIn, TikTok, and Instagram to share resources and insights about career-related advice ranging from compensation negotiation to their own interview stories. Both left their corporate jobs to turn content creation and career consulting, their passions, into fulltime careers with impact as the top priority.

It took a lot of time and patience, but the leap to content creation paid off. From receiving over 50 million content impressions every month to being featured on *Forbes*, *Business Insider*, and *Fortune*, Jonathan and Jerry's continuous journeys as creators have catapulted them into the spotlight and led them on the journey of impact they sought to pursue. Every day, they are tagged in new success stories of individuals who received job offers after using their resources or following their advice.

What started out as a few LinkedIn posts five years ago has ballooned into an international resource that has helped thousands of job seekers land their dream jobs and cultivated a global community of over two million members.

"The best way I describe content creation is to imagine if you're talking to a million people every single day," Jonathan said emphatically. "Inevitably, one of those conversations could lead to a business opportunity. One of those could lead to a potentially life-changing moment." Because Jonathan and Jerry see content creation as a conversation with everyone on the planet, they are convinced the benefits of being a creator are immeasurable.

Part II of this book, "Self-Made Success," delves deeper into how the Creator Revolution has given us a new reality: one in which you can design your own future. You no longer have to be subject to existing societal hierarchies or structures. Instead, you can pursue your passions, control your own narrative and outcome, and have greater autonomy in doing so. While being a creator is by no means an easy path, it can pave the way for new and unforeseen opportunities.

PURSUING YOUR PASSIONS

The word "passion" is derived from the Latin root *pati-*, which means "to suffer." Today, the word "passion" generally refers to "a strong feeling of enthusiasm or excitement for something or about doing something," as *Merriam-Webster* defines. (Perhaps it is something you are so enthusiastic about you are willing to suffer for it.)

In Chapter 2, we learned how the term "passion economy" was coined to describe the phenomenon of how individuals, particularly content creators, could now monetize their individuality and hobbies (i.e. "passions") through creative work. The growth and infrastructure of the passion economy underpins much of the Creator Revolution.

In particular, creating content has unlocked the power to pursue your passions as a career. Dominic Panganiban, better known online as Domics, is an animation artist and creator who exemplifies this.

Growing up, Dominic always enjoyed drawing. His parents, on the other hand, did not want him to pursue a career as an artist for fear of its uncertainty and lack of stability. As a compromise to his family, he studied architecture in college. But he wasn't happy—he didn't like architecture, why was he subjecting himself to it?

As a result, he sought creative outlets outside of what he studied. In 2010, halfway through college, Dominic started a web comic on microblogging social network Tumblr. His first post was a black and white comic with seven panels, where one character rapidly spins their head instead of performing a "headspin," the breakdancing move. The caption was simple: "Thinking 'bout starting a web comic. Maybe this'll be the first of many :]".

That day, a new creator was born.

By the time he graduated from university two years later, he had amassed an audience of over 100,000 followers on Tumblr (Burgin, 2018). If you scroll through his Tumblr today, you would have to navigate through seventy-one pages of posts before you get to his very first post. With each passing week, you could see his posts become more complex; nuanced character designs, colored illustrations, and detailed shading emerged over time.

With his growing audience and accumulated experience, Dominic wanted to fulfill greater visions and ideas for his comics. This naturally culminated in learning the art of animating illustrations. From there he was inspired to start a YouTube channel to post his animations, which he launched in August of 2012. His first video on YouTube, similar to his simple start on Tumblr, was a mere fourteen-second animation clip; in the video, his voiceover pokes fun at how he struggles to pronounce the word "rural."

His existing audience followed him from Tumblr to YouTube, and he gained many new fans on the video platform. Since his first video nine years ago, almost every animation video he has published has received over a million views. Dominic discovered his niche was storytelling animation videos, in which he tells anecdotes from his life through a voiceover overlaid with his animations, ranging from stories about interacting with grade school crushes to buying used products from strangers online.

Today the Domics YouTube channel has gathered over 7.4 million subscribers and 1 billion views. Not only has he achieved great success as an individual creator, he was one of the earliest pioneers of animated storytelling on YouTube that a generation of successful animation creators like Jaiden Animations, James Rallison (TheOdd1sOut), and

Dennise Casurra (CypherDen) have since followed in the footsteps of.

Needless to say, Dominic never ended up putting his architecture degree to use. Instead, he was able to launch his fulltime career pursuing his ultimate passion of art with complete autonomy and ownership due to the existence of and access to creator platforms like Tumblr and YouTube.

Last year, YouTube creators Colin and Samir polled their subscribers to see how much they valued their passion and autonomy. Out of over 12,000 respondents, 66 percent said they would accept a pay cut if it meant they could pursue their passion fulltime (Ophelia, 2021). Many of the creators we have seen and will see in this book began creating content to follow their passions. The path of a creator differs from other existing routes in that you can do what you love and potentially create opportunities out of your passions, all while exercising your decision-making autonomy.

Ask yourself, what are your passions? How can you impart your knowledge and love for them to the rest of the world?

CREATING YOUR PERSONAL BRAND

Jess Li was on her way to graduating college and entering investment banking when her friend roped her into writing Medium articles about entrepreneurs at her alma mater. She never imagined she would publish writing online: she had never liked writing and humanities classes in school, plus English was her second language.

Slowly but surely, she began to enjoy publishing content online, particularly when it came to sharing insights and advice from her own experiences to assist others interested in the field of entrepreneurship. As her writing audience grew, something unexpected happened for her: doors she had never sought out magically opened. The founders of the start-up Elpha, a professional network for women, invited her to lead their content strategy. As her Medium articles gained traction, she received inbound requests to write for notable publications such as *TechCrunch* and companies such as Pinduoduo.

Even though she had only been a fulltime working professional for a few years, Jess was frequently invited to speak as an expert in entrepreneurship. "Once you have that initial pool of experience, credibility, and brand, other things kind of come to you more," she explained to me. "For me, content creation was how the flywheel started, so to speak."

Jess is one of many creators who realized by creating content, you can build your own brand and credibility, which can lead to new opportunities. Actor and influencer Blake Michael told *Forbes* "everyone has a brand and social media allows us to amplify it," and there's no better time to do so than now, during the Creator Revolution.

In 2020, Meagan Loyst, then a wide-eyed twenty-three-year-old, stepped into her new job as a venture capital (VC) investor. She quickly realized she was nearly ten years younger than everyone else on the team. There she was, a young, no-name investor fresh out of college, without a strong network of connections that was so critical for succeeding in the industry and without the credibility to persuade start-ups to believe in her as an investor. So she asked herself, how could she differentiate herself?

CREATOR TIP:
How do I build my personal brand?

In building your personal brand, the creators I've interviewed have given the following advice:

1. **Find your niche.**
   Maybe you're an expert at giving career advice. Or maybe you know all possible Starbucks flavor combos. There is absolutely nothing that is too niche. Ask yourself: what do you enjoy doing? What would you like to share with others? Once you find it, lean into it and start exploring. See how your audience responds and what feedback they give you.

2. **Be authentic.**
   Don't try to guess what other people want to see from you. Let your own voice shine through. It's very easy for others to sense when you are not being authentic, which causes audiences to lose trust. Being genuine and real is a great way for your audience to truly connect with you.

3. **Be consistent with your messaging and branding.**
   Try to centralize around your brand's identity. This will help people to know what to expect from you and what value they receive from following your content.

4. **Just get started!**
   The hardest step to building your personal brand is getting started. Take a deep breath, choose a platform, and just hit publish. Then the hardest part will soon be over.

She turned to the obvious best answer: creating content.

Meagan dug out her old Twitter account, which had around fifty followers at the time, and began engaging with interesting people she wanted to chat more with and learn from. One night, wondering if there were other young investors out there like her, she tweeted, "Any investors born '96 or later? I've been thinking a lot about Gen Z investing in Gen Z. Would love to compile key themes, [favorite companies], personal stories, etc. with other Gen Z investors. Who should I chat with?"

Little did she know, her late-night thought-turned-tweet had piqued the interest of many. After receiving over one hundred replies on her tweet, Meagan scheduled seventy-one conversations with peers all around the world and published an article documenting her findings. The article—her first article—accumulated over 800 "claps" and 10,000 reads and kickstarted her brand as the pioneer of Generation Z venture capital investing, with many crowning her as the "Queen of Gen Z VC."

Meagan leaned into her personal brand and started the "Gen Z VCs" Slack community, which today has grown to not just a massive following of 14,000 participants, but also to an entire movement dedicated to empowering young voices and collaborations. In less than a year, she successfully cemented her personal brand as a Gen Z investor and established herself as *the* voice of the demographic. She rocketed from 50 to over 30,000 followers on Twitter and staked her place in *Forbes*'s prestigious 30 Under 30 list. When media outlets seek opinions and thoughts about emerging Gen Z trends and products, Meagan is now the de facto voice and has been featured in *Business Insider* (over 12 times), *The Washington Post*, *Cosmopolitan*, Bloomberg TV, and other notable news publications.

A tweet, an article, and a Slack community turned Meagan's life upside-down, thrusting her into the spotlight as a creator, community leader, and role model. This all stemmed from her desire to create content and use it to develop her personal brand. "The barriers to creation are just so minimal today—anyone and everyone can build an audience and build a following. It's just never been easier, and I'm a perfect example of that," Meagan reflected during our conversation.

More people than ever are using creator platforms and social media to build their own brand. In doing so, you can establish your credibility, control the narrative, and raise awareness around you and your insights or value-add, thereby broadening your reach and opening new doors for opportunities.

It's a good time to start brainstorming: how will you start building your personal brand?

ELEVATING YOURSELF TO THE NEXT LEVEL

It's January 2009, and a high school adolescent boy is speaking into his computer. "I bought a new laptop and it's an HP Pavilion dv7t Media Center, so of course I've got the media center remote with it. Quite a nice remote," he narrates as he holds the remote up to his blurry webcam. He then uploads his review on YouTube.

A little over a decade later, he's no longer in high school, but he is still posting videos on YouTube. This individual is Marques Brownlee, one of the most well-known technology content creators in the world. With over 15 million subscribers and 2.9 billion total views on his YouTube channel, Marques reviews the latest smartphones, laptops, tablets, electric cars, and any other electronics you can think of.

Over the years, he has interviewed many of the most prominent names in technology, including Elon Musk, Bill Gates, Satya Nadella, Mark Zuckerberg, and Sundar Pichai. He has also spoken with celebrities outside of the field, including former basketball star Kobe Bryant, former US president Barack Obama, and actor Will Smith. In 2015, Marques became the first YouTuber to be invited to any of Apple's press events when he received an invitation to the launch of a new MacBook device.

It is easy to admire Marques and marvel at his successes. But his climb to celebrity status came from his deliberate choices, dedication, and diligence. Unlike most other fifteen-year-olds, he chose to spend his free time posting tech-related videos because he enjoyed sharing his knowledge and thoughts. He posted his hundredth video less than two months after launching his channel, an incredible milestone for a creator of any age. Today, his channel has published over 1,400 videos; additionally, he has launched a few other channels, a podcast, a YouTube original series, merchandise, and other ventures (Patel, 2021).

Marques pursued his passions and shared his love with fans all over the world by creating content about what he enjoyed sharing knowledge about—technology. His consistent content then established his credibility and brand, and his following and visibility grew as a result. Taking advantage of the Creator Revolution opened the floodgates of opportunities for him to speak with the largest names in the world and cement a fulltime career reviewing consumer electronic gadgets. "It felt like a long time coming," he said to *The Ringer* in 2016. "It just gives you a sense of legitimacy. I'm around the tech blogs and *The New York Times* of the world, because [YouTube] matters." His content has enabled him to blaze new trails for his own career and the millions of tech consumers around the world who await his reviews and entrust their gadget purchasing decisions to his advice.

We can all learn from Marques. After all, he, too, began with a humble first video in front of a blurry webcam.

> Creating content bestows the following superpowers:
> 1. Pursuing one's passions, which allows for greater autonomy.
> 2. Creating a personal brand, which expands one's influence.
> 3. Increasing visibility, which opens new doors.

CASE STUDY:
Ludwig Ahgren

On a sunny Sunday afternoon in Los Angeles, Ludwig Ahgren turned his camera on and began another Twitch livestream.

He did not turn off the camera until thirty-one days later.

For that entire month, Ludwig broadcasted nearly every moment of his life. Not just playing video games, as one might expect from his usual livestreams. Instead, his fans also watched him cook dinners, fix a refrigerator, work out in the gym, sleep, host movie nights, and even shower (while donning shorts) on camera. No matter what time I opened my Twitch app, I always saw Ludwig's stream atop the list of live channels.

What started out as an experiment for Ludwig quickly spiraled into a historic moment. It is not uncommon for Twitch streamers to hold a "subathon", which is a short period of time when a creator streams nonstop and performs specific actions in order to reach a subscriber goal. Essentially, creators trade actions for subscriptions ("subs"). For example, a creator could promise their fans that they will play a new game at 1,000 subs, eat a dried tarantula at 1,500 subs, and dye their hair a color of fans' choice at 3,000 subs. Alternatively, each subscription could increase the timer by an increment, incentivizing fans to extend the stream longer.

Ludwig's subathon fell into the second category, with each new sub adding ten seconds to the clock. However, he did something different: he let the timer run indefinitely, believing it would expire sometime within the next two days. Two days turned into three, which turned into five, and quickly the stream turned viral. Viewers never wanted it to end, so they kept subscribing or "gifting" subs to other fans, extending his stream until Ludwig finally ended it a month later. By then he had broken the all-time record for most subscriptions on Twitch at 282,000. In comparison, he only had 1,730 subscriptions on the day before his subathon started, according to *The Verge*.

What Ludwig did went far beyond documenting his life in meticulously curated and edited videos. As evidenced by his astronomical viewership, his subathon cultivated such a high appeal by generating what appeared to be a deeper connection with his audience. Instead of being distant observers, fans viewed the subathon as a collective community experience they actively participated and had a voice in.

"The weirdest thing is every time I wake up, it feels like it gets bigger and bigger," Ludwig told *The New York Times*. If he had not decided to start streaming one day, Ludwig would have never catapulted into record-breaking heights, signed a new exclusive contract with YouTube, or even been featured in this book—all of which began from just having an internet connection.

CHAPTER 7

Creators as Entrepreneurs

*"If you are always trying to be normal,
you will never know how amazing you can be."*

—MAYA ANGELOU, POET, AUTHOR, AND ACTIVIST

Michelle Phan's life looked very different fifteen years ago. Having grown up in a single mother household and barely scraping together enough money for college, Michelle was twenty years old and waiting tables.

Today, she has inspired a generation of beauty gurus and founded a company worth 800 million dollars.

Back in 2007, she spent her spare time writing a personal blog about her favorite hobby: makeup. "I had a blog, and I was blogging about different tutorials… A lot of girls were asking for me to write one up [about makeup]," Michelle explained to *The Insider* in 2012. "So I posted it on my blog and then afterwards I thought, *Why not just film it?*"

So in May of that year, she uploaded her first makeup tutorial video, "Natural Looking Makeup Tutorial," to You-Tube. More videos followed, covering every design imaginable: makeup for glasses (4.4 million views), eyes inspired by anime characters (8 million views), a Snow White transformation (12 million views), two Lady Gaga music video-inspired looks (90 million views combined), and hundreds more.

Chosen by YouTube as one of the first creators to monetize their content, Michelle quit her job when the advertising revenue she earned from her videos matched her waitress wages. Her popularity continued to surge, and she became the first woman to hit one million YouTube subscribers three years later. The same year, French luxury cosmetics line Lancôme appointed her as their official video makeup artist and ambassador (Morris, 2014). At the pinnacle of her YouTube career, she had over nine million subscribers (Hou, 2019). Her videos have received over one billion views to date.

"I promised [my mother] I would find a way to take care of the family. I just never imagined it would be through YouTube," she revealed in a heartfelt interview with *Glamour*.

As transcendent as her rise as a creator already was, Michelle's journey did not end there. In 2011, she co-founded a monthly beauty product subscription service later branded as Ipsy. It raised over 100 million dollars in funding and was valued at 800 million dollars four years later (Griffith, 2015). In 2013, she collaborated with L'Oréal to launch EM Cosmetics; she purchased the brand back from L'Oréal and relaunched it in 2017 to focus the products on comfort, texture, and a diverse shade range (Lukas, 2021). A year later, she co-founded peer-to-peer music marketplace start-up Thematic (Weiss, 2018).

Her path from waitress to creator to entrepreneur was far from straightforward. It's incredible to see how she pioneered the era of beauty influencers and elevated her role as a creator into something much greater. While Michelle took multiple extended hiatuses from video creation during the formative years of her businesses' growth and rarely creates content anymore, her experience and expertise as a creator aided her success in building her businesses and becoming an entrepreneur.

In Chapter 6, we learned about how creators are shaping their own future and opening new doors. In this chapter, we will hear more about how creators are opening a unique type of door: the door to entrepreneurship.

CREATOR VS. ENTREPRENEUR

Who comes to mind when you hear the word "entrepreneur"? Perhaps fearless visionaries like Steve Jobs. Trailblazers driven to create their own future like Katrina Lake. Unusual risk-takers like Mark Zuckerberg.

The *Merriam-Webster Dictionary* defines an entrepreneur as "a person who starts a business and is willing to risk loss in order to make money." On a high level, creators are not the same as entrepreneurs. They are distinct roles with different actions: creators publish content while entrepreneurs generally sell a service or product.

Nonetheless, the spirits of a creator and entrepreneur are quite similar—and we see that entrepreneurial spirit shine through in Twitch streamer Alex Deng.

During our conversation, Alex described himself as someone who has been "gaming [his] whole life." However, he struggled to find a job that was related to his passion for gaming, so he pursued a career in finance. He worked in venture capital and private equity roles, which required him to understand, evaluate, and invest in businesses. Years later, when he landed the position of partnership manager at Team Liquid, one of the world's leading competitive esports (electronic sports) and gaming organizations, he thought that would be the closest he'd ever get to the pinnacle of his gaming ambitions.

Surrounded by so many professional gamers and content creators, he felt inspired to stream his gameplay on Twitch, adopting the online alias "Birdyfood." Given his background in finance and venture capital, he approached streaming with a logical mindset.

"Every viewer is a sale I must close," Alex emphasized. He focuses on his follower count and follower count growth rate as his key performance indicators, a term commonly used by entrepreneurs to refer to quantifiable metrics for tracking a company's overall performance.

For many creators, myself included, the beginning of the creator journey is often slow. Most of us published our first piece of content for fun and spent the first few months learning and experimenting. In contrast, Alex took a methodical and deliberate approach. He treated streaming like owning a business, and it paid off. After one year of streaming, he was named a Twitch partner, a designation only 1 percent of the 2 million active Twitch streamers achieve.

While Alex did not start out as an entrepreneur, he carries an entrepreneurial mindset as a creator. This approach makes sense when you compare the milestones both creators and entrepreneurs have adopted.

1. **Creating value for their customers**: Businesses create value through the services and/or products they are selling. Creators generate value through their content, whether it be entertainment, knowledge, resources, tutorials, and so on.

2. **Finding customers**: A business cannot exist without customers. Likewise, a creator has no reach or impact without an audience.

3. **Growing their audience and presence**: This ties in closely with the first milestone. Neither entrepreneurs nor creators can achieve long-term success unless they expand their customer base.

4. **Building brand loyalty and trust**: Once a sizable audience has been established, both entrepreneurs and creators need to keep them. They do that by catering to their needs, which builds and cements loyalty and trust in the business or creator's brand.

5. **Making money as the end goal**: It goes without saying profit is the primary goal for businesses. For many creators, the ultimate goal is to monetize their content in order to sustain themselves and/or finance future projects and content. They must be creative in how they do so—crowdfunding, merchandise sales, subscriptions, online courses, etc. (This will be discussed in more detail in Chapter 8.)

A key component of *Merriam-Webster*'s definition mentioned entrepreneurs are "willing to risk loss." That naturally leads us to creators, a role that requires risking one's time and money to get started. For some creators who want to take it to the next level, they may quit their day jobs to pursue their passion fulltime.

"The line between being a creator and entrepreneur is very blurry," Sandy Lin told me. A creator herself, Sandy has founded several businesses and currently instructs a TikTok (@bysandylin) audience of over 300,000 on how to monetize as a creator. Inspired by her experiences as an entrepreneur and creator, she also founded Small Business Tips, a community-centered collective dedicated to empowering the next generation of entrepreneurs, and Creobase, an all-in-one platform to help creators monetize and manage brand partnerships. She explained, "Creators are, in fact, running their own operations, creating scripts, designing content, managing their monetization and taxes…So much of that is like what an entrepreneur does in a sense. They just view themselves very differently."

Being a creator is by no means a guaranteed career path, but it has a better chance of being one if you approach the craft like running your own business. Both entrepreneurs and content creators experience similar pivotal milestones and mentalities in their respective roles. This resemblance can be taken to the next level as creators put themselves in the shoes of entrepreneurs.

CREATORS AS ENTREPRENEURS

For most people, getting fired from a job is *not* a cause for celebration. However, for Ohio University senior Tony Piloseno, being fired ended up being the catalyst for launching his own successful paint business.

Tony (@tonesterpaints) began posting paint mixing videos in December of 2019. His first TikTok, a brief eleven-second clip, showed him pouring two streams of paint together into a bucket of existing paint, creating a stunning orange, yellow, and green gradient. Then a part-time employee at Sherwin-Williams, Tony captioned his video, "Come buy some paint @ sherwin".

As fans became fascinated with the mesmerizing art of paint mixing, his views and influence kept climbing. By his sixth video, a brief explanation of how a gallon of paint receives its color, he had finally crossed the virality benchmark of one million views on a video.

Tony thought his account was a clear mechanism for promoting Sherwin-Williams's presence and marketing, particularly to a younger audience. In an interview with *BuzzFeed News*, he revealed he had created a pitch deck "to show the company how TikTok has a younger base" and "to basically develop brand awareness through TikTok," eventually presenting his learnings and ideas to corporate headquarters.

But Sherwin-Williams held a different opinion. Between his marketing proposal and the numerous calls they had received about experimental paint mixing (all inspired by Tony's videos), the company was on high alert. Seven months after he started posting TikToks to promote his company's brand, Tony was fired by Sherwin-Williams. They claimed he violated many company policies, such as filming these videos during working hours and using company equipment for them.

Despite getting fired, Tony continued to film himself mixing paint. At the time, he had already amassed over a million followers on TikTok. His videos grew in creative variety, combining user-requested color shades and producing different aesthetics, such as a yin-yang pattern or the celestial look of a galaxy. He fielded job offers from other paint competitors like Behr and Benjamin Moore, eventually joining Florida Paints as a sales associate with the stipulation he could use their manufacturing equipment to launch his own paint line. "I chose to work with Florida Paints because they were going to help me start my own brand of paint products and color," Tony explained to *The Publish Press*. "It's a smaller paint company, so I'm able to work more closely with the people running the organization [and] have better communication and more creative freedom."

Today, Tony has over 2.5 million followers combined across TikTok and YouTube. While he continues to produce content on a regular basis, his primary focus is on his business: Tonester Paints. Selling and shipping hand-crafted and customized colors, Tony now spends his time not just sharing, but now making and selling what he loves with his audience: paints.

It was Tony's beginnings as a creator that led him to spread the art of paint mixing, partner with a paint corporation, and launch his own business. His content and creativity allowed him to rise above and beyond his firing, granting him the opportunity to partner with brands and successfully launch his own paint business.

The arduous path of entrepreneurship has always required the founder to cement their skill and credibility before receiving customer interest, investment, and partnerships. Tony unlocked the key to this path by creating content, thereby establishing his own customer market: the market of those interested in mixing paints.

Nastassia Ponomarenko, much like Tony, was rather young when she began posting videos about makeup and fitness on YouTube. Five years later, at the age of twenty-one, she is not only a creator with over 1.4 million followers across social media—she has also launched a fitness apparel brand worth seven figures.

An avid fan of other beauty creators like RCLBeauty and Bethany Mota, Nastassia was inspired to document her own journey on camera. She started posting regular content about her beauty and fitness journey on YouTube and Instagram, growing a following that has stayed with her over the years. A year after launching her channel, Nastassia already had over 100 thousand subscribers. Around that time, a fitness company approached her and asked if she would be willing to sell their workout guides for a set commission price. That was the first time she realized she could earn money as a creator, and she agreed wholeheartedly.

Thanks to this newfound revelation and her growing fanbase, Nastassia has been financially independent since the age of seventeen.

Another year passed, and British fitness apparel brand Gym Shark went viral on social media. Seeing that phenomenon as someone who loved fitness and fashion, Nastassia decided to launch her own fitness apparel brand. "I took some of that profit I'd made, and then I started my own business," she recalled to me. She realized being a creator was a natural progression toward becoming an entrepreneur. "I already had those first customers lined up. That's a huge plus to being a creator—you have those early customers who love you and want to pay."

This isn't to say being a creator was the deciding factor in her becoming an entrepreneur: "Let's say, you know, if I wasn't a creator, would I still be building businesses? I think the answer could be yes…but [by being a creator] you get those early customers. It becomes easier to build brands. You have that audience, and you can use it."

No matter what path led her to entrepreneurship, Nastassia recognized the value of having an existing following and using it as her customer base. It is much easier to build a company and brand by tapping into one's audience rather than starting from scratch to find the early customers, figure out how to create value for them, build brand loyalty, and so on. Nastassia's business thrived, and she is now building her third venture, a social fitness start-up.

Michelle established a cosmetic empire, Tony spring boarded himself into a paints business, and Nastassia launched an apparel line and fitness technology start-up.

By building and growing their audience, creators can build long-term, sustainable businesses. Being a creator not only offers autonomy, new opportunities, and a potential path to stardom—it can jumpstart the journey to becoming an entrepreneur.

PLATFORMS AS INVESTORS

Across the table from entrepreneurs sit investors, the individuals who have the power to decide which businesses receive more funding and support. Investors scout talented entrepreneurs and founders, conduct research on their growth potential, and carefully select who to invest money, time, and mentorship into. Naturally, the companies with the most resources are the most likely to succeed.

To round out the creator-entrepreneur analogy, we must also consider the investor counterpart: creator platforms.

A former member of the Creator and Artist Partnerships team at YouTube, Jad Esber worked to increase and scale creator growth in emerging markets. In our conversation, he recalled how the team "operated like angel investors," investing time to support the growth of high potential creators. For Jad and his team, this meant continuously tracking a variety of metrics of YouTube creators as signals to help spot emergent talent on the platform.

YouTube is not the only creator platform looking for and "investing" in high potential creators. Last year, LinkedIn announced they wanted to bring more creators to the platform through a 25-million-dollar creator fund, a creator accelerator, and other smaller initiatives (Lunden, 2021). While writing this book, I received a message from a LinkedIn creator manager asking if I'd be interested in joining their Creator Program. This was one of their newly launched initiatives that involved coaching, instruction, and mentorship on how to best use LinkedIn to grow as a creator on the platform. They saw my announcement about writing this book and invited me to participate and use the platform to grow my book audience.

Curious to learn more, I decided to join their program. I was impressed by the direct access to help. Whenever I wanted to discuss content ideas, get feedback on my content, or ask about anything else, I could instantly set up time to chat with my assigned creator manager. They also periodically sent me content ideas and prompts to write about. If one of my posts was relevant to a prompt, I sent my creator manager my post; it would then soon be added to a public LinkedIn newsletter that was sent to the inboxes of millions of users.

I was surprised at how much having that direct line of communication changed my approach to content creation on LinkedIn, a site where I had rarely published content on previously. Through seminars and office hours, I was taught tips and tricks that were optimal for the platform. I had an endless supply of content ideas, which was something I had previously struggled with. Anytime I posted, LinkedIn was on my side helping me try to amplify my content and achieve my goals. All of these were actions I would not have undertaken if it had not been for the platform's "investment" and support.

It is important to note investment in creators is no longer limited to platforms. In Chapter 8 and Chapter 12, we will look at new ways to support and invest in a creator as a venture capitalist, as a creator, and as a fan.

The Creator Revolution has ushered in a new era of creators stepping into the role of entrepreneurs. It works in both directions: creators have a direct path to become entrepreneurs, and creator platforms are investors on the lookout for emerging talents. Not all creators become entrepreneurs, but being a creator makes it easier to do so.

> Being a creator lends a natural path to being an entrepreneur.

CHAPTER 8

Creators as Businesses

"The best way to predict the future is to create it."
—PETER DRUCKER, AUTHOR AND BUSINESS VISIONARY

Much to his mother's chagrin, eighteen-year-old Jimmy Donaldson decided to drop out of college to pursue his dream of making it big on YouTube. After posting videos on the platform since he was twelve years old, Jimmy was positive it was only a matter of time before he cracked the code to virality.

A few months later, he did.

In a video *Bloomberg* described years later as "an oddly mesmerizing performance," Jimmy sat down in a black leather chair and began filming himself mumbling numbers for over 40 hours straight, starting from zero and slowly murmuring his way to 100,000. The video, titled "I Counted to 100,000!", skyrocketed to five million views in five days and became a viral hit despite totaling nearly twenty-four hours in length. Sure, he may have repeated a couple of numbers, even missed a few numbers here and there, but it wasn't about accuracy. The incredible stunt captivated the YouTube audience with its sheer absurdity. Every kid fantasizes of counting to 100,000 but never succeeds—here was a man crazy enough to actually do it.

More outrageous stunts followed, one viral smash hit after another: "Watching Dance Till You're Dead for 10 Hours," "Reading the Longest English Word (190,000 Characters)," "Watching It's Everyday Bro For 10 Hours Straight," and so on, each garnering tens of millions of views. Jimmy then began to capitalize on the audience's fascination with extravagant stunts and numbers by shifting that focus to something that was guaranteed to draw attention instantaneously: money.

After he received his first YouTube sponsorship deal of ten thousand dollars, Jimmy pondered, "How can I transform this money into something good?" Instead of keeping the money for himself, he decided to give it all away while still leveraging it as content to earn more money for future acts of charity. He gave away tens of thousands of dollars to his subscribers, homeless people, pizza delivery drivers, waitresses, random online creators, and many more ordinary individuals, filming their reactions in doing so and racking up tens of millions of views each time. Jimmy repeatedly demonstrated he knew the pathway to virality inside and out, front and back, regardless of how YouTube's algorithm evolved over time.

But he didn't just stop there. Jimmy, better known today by his online name "MrBeast," completely shattered barriers and redefined the possibilities a creator could establish as their own brand.

Jimmy decided to deepen his focus on philanthropy as his audience and numbers grew. He continued to gift money to participants in his video content, sometimes giving away millions of dollars at a time, but other initiatives—such as raising enough money to plant 20 million trees, removing 30 million pounds of waste, and aiding Hurricane Ida survivors—required far more planning and intensive capital.

So a slew of ventures ensued, all with the goal of diversifying his business into as many revenue channels as possible in order to both pour into his philanthropic efforts and better his content. Jimmy announced the MrBeast Burger franchise, which partnered with hundreds of ghost kitchens across the United States to produce his menu and sell his branded burgers. While I was writing this book, he launched a second food venture, a line of chocolate bars called Feastables. He solidified his charitable efforts by establishing the Beast Philanthropy nonprofit, which "exists to leverage the power of social media platforms and raise funds to alleviate hunger, homelessness, and unemployment" worldwide, according to their website's mission statement.

The MrBeast Burger app skyrocketed to the second most popular free app in the App Store just two days after its release. Similarly, two years later, over 25 million people watched his announcement video of the new candy line two days after the launch of his new chocolate brand (Doyle, 2022). This is a beautiful demonstration of how Jimmy's influence has extended far beyond his role as a creator, or even as the individual behind his ventures—he is a business in and of himself.

"Instead of following a brand, fans today follow a creator who will launch their own brand, because they care about the creator," entrepreneur and TikTok marketing creator Jules Montgomery (@itxmejules) told me in an interview. Jimmy has built up such a robust community with his outlandish stunts and philanthropic initiatives that his fans choose to support him and whatever he sets out to create—because he *is* the brand.

In the previous chapter, we heard stories of creators who took the leap to launch their own businesses. Now we will take it one step further: not only are they leading businesses, creators *are* their own businesses. These two chapters are inextricably intertwined: we will see that many creators in both chapters are simultaneously budding entrepreneurs and thriving brands. This chapter will specifically highlight how creators follow the business development cycle to position themselves as the most valuable brands of the future.

IDEATION, DEVELOPMENT, AND GROWTH

A full business development process consists of five stages: ideation, development, growth, commercialization, and exit. The same process applies to creators, as we can see in Figure 8.1.

While it is easy to marvel at the success his MrBeast franchise has amounted to today, Jimmy did not strike gold on his first few videos—or even his first few years.

His earliest videos on YouTube, posted over ten years ago, were short clips of himself playing games like *Minecraft* and *Pokémon Showdown*. In between, he dabbled with other topics, including a series of videos estimating the net worth of popular YouTubers. Unlike his videos today, where he is the central personality of every video and his face is plastered across each thumbnail, Jimmy physically appeared in very few of his early videos.

Around 2015, he saw a slow rise in subscribers as a result of a series of videos known as "Worst Intros," in which he mocked and showcased the worst YouTube introductions he found on the site. He reached thirty thousand subscribers around mid-2016, over four years since he began and half a year away from his viral moment.

The first step for any business is **ideation**. For a creator, that means brainstorming content topics, ideas, and goals. Reiterating ideas we first saw in Chapter 1, it is critical to

Figure 8.1: The business development process as applied to creators.

determine the goal and value you want to provide your audience early in the process. For Jimmy, his value clearly was to entertain. He compiled gaming highlights, rounded up amusing YouTube introductions, and speculated about the wealth of the biggest YouTube creators.

Ideation goes hand-in-hand with the next step, **development**. Once a creator has established their overarching objectives, they must validate and refine their content strategy by publishing content, soliciting feedback, and iterating.

A business must achieve product-market fit, which occurs when the company's product has been proven to satisfy a strong market demand—or, in simpler words, they truly make something people want. Similarly, a creator must devote time to seeking **creator-market fit**, the perfect "aha!" moment that has proven effective value for both the creator and their audience. Venture capitalist Li Jin defines creator-market fit as "the union between content creation, audience, and business model." Specifically for creators to consider whether they have reached this milestone, she poses these three questions:

1. "Do I enjoy making this?"
2. "Do people want this?"
3. "Can I sustain myself?"

Jimmy's creator-market fit moment was the viral success of counting aloud to 100,000. He recognized the YouTube audience's desire for extraordinary and increasingly outlandish stunts, especially when unfathomable amounts of money were involved.

After achieving creator-market fit, the creator should stick to their now-validated content strategy and focus on audience and community **growth**. The faster you scale, the more value you can provide to your audience, and the more you can bolster your brand.

Jimmy has continued to follow his tried-and-true content strategy five years after his viral hit. At the time of writing this, his three most recent videos were "World's Most Dangerous Escape Room!", "Extreme $1,000,000 Hide and Seek", and "$1,000,000 Influencer Tournament!" All three videos feature eye-popping content and unbelievable titles, leveraging a superlative or promising a million dollars, and it worked—each video has received over forty million views. With over ninety million subscribers and fifteen billion views on his main YouTube channel as of early 2022, it is safe to say Jimmy has outperformed all expectations and crystallized his place in history as a creator to remember. And he did so by devoting time to ideation, development, and growth—the first three steps in the creator business development process—with zeal and consistency.

COMMERCIALIZATION

What if you pushed yourself to do things *no one else* dared to try?

This is the question Eugene Lee Yang, Keith Habersberger, Ned Fulmer, and Zach Kornfeld pondered before dedicating their next eight years (and beyond) to investigating it in depth for a global audience of millions.

An online comedy quartet formed in 2014 at American media company BuzzFeed, the "Try Guys" created a video series where they tried anything for entertainment, accumulating billions of views on their videos. Their most popular video, "The Try Guys Try Drag For The First Time," has amassed over 37 million views since its release.

In early 2018, they left BuzzFeed to launch their own independent production company, 2nd Try LLC. Later that June, they launched a new YouTube channel. Since then, they have gathered over 7.5 million subscribers and almost 2 billion views on their channel.

"We've been using the Try Guys to unlock a lot of creative dreams and ambitions that the four of us have had together and as individuals," Zach revealed in an interview with *Digiday*. But wanting more creative autonomy was only one of the reasons for their departure. They also admitted they wanted more than what Buzzfeed could pay them. By establishing their own production company, they gained greater control and diversification of their **commercialization** strategy.

Three years later, the Try Guys' revenue streams span direct payments (via YouTube AdSense), branded advertising on videos and podcasts, merchandise, sales of a *New York Times* #1 bestselling book, tour tickets, product lines (hot sauces, tea, and a cookbook), and Patreon memberships, where they currently have over 3,700 supporters. They even landed a deal for an upcoming show on the Food Network with a similar concept to their popular video series *Without a Recipe*, in which they attempt to make food such as ice cream, bagels, and pizza without accessing any instructions (Leiber, 2021).

In their years of producing and publishing content, the Try Guys had already figured out their niche, refined their content to achieve creator-market fit, and built a sizable following. They capitalized on their customer base to build their own company to scale their profits to new heights, officially crossing the bridge from creators to an impressive media brand in their own right.

In a blog post announcing YouTube's priorities for 2021, the platform's CEO Susan Wojcicki noted, "Creators are building next generation media companies that impact the economy's overall success." The Try Guys succeeded in transforming themselves into a media company, one with multiple revenue streams and a blossoming community that is still growing on a daily basis.

Today, creator business models mostly revolve around the following five key monetization mechanisms:

- **Platform payments**: Creators receive direct payments from the creator platform. Examples include YouTube's AdSense program, TikTok's Creator Fund, Roblox's Developer Exchange program, and Pinterest's Creator Rewards.
- **Digital memberships**: Fans support their favorite creators by making consistent and small subscription payments in exchange for access to their exclusive communities and customized perks.
- **Crowdfunding and donations**: Creators can start crowdfunding campaigns or request donations (also called tips or gifts) as a means of additional audience support.
- **Branded sponsorships and partnerships**: Corporations and brands can partner with creators to produce sponsored content and collaborations.
- **Products and services, often related to the creator's niche**: For example, cooking creators often launch their own kitchenware, salt and seasoning product lines, and online recipe bundles. Successful beauty influencers have followed in Michelle Phan's footsteps to establish new makeup lines and brands. Gaming creators sell clothing merchandise as well as personalized gaming gear like keyboards, mice, and mousepads.

Going forward, we will also see this extend to monetizing more involved and interactive experiences in the **metaverse**, a virtual world that exists beyond the one in which we live. I had the pleasure of speaking with Annie Zhang, host of the *Hello Metaverse* podcast and a product manager at Roblox, a platform that enables anyone to create digital social games and experiences. Over the last few years, Annie has witnessed a surge in interest from creators hoping to add functionalities in the metaverse: "We are beginning to get a lot of demand from influencers who ask, 'Hey, what's a cooler and more immersive way for us to engage with our audiences?' So we're starting to build these immersive interactive worlds for influencers as well." From developing tools for creators to host virtual concerts and premium fan meetups, to assisting them to sell digital merchandise, "We're only just scraping the tip of the iceberg," Annie predicts.

There is a lot of creative potential in the realm of commercialization—perhaps you will discover a new method and pave the way for other creators to follow.

CASE STUDY:
Vanessa Ideh Adekoya

With over 230,000 subscribers and 4.2 million views in less than a year since launching her channel "Launch To Wealth," Nigerian YouTuber Vanessa Ideh Adekoya makes the creator journey look easy. In reality, it took time and iteration. Her first YouTube channel's strategy was to create content surrounding trending topics. For her second channel, she improved from her learnings and niched down, focusing on finance education for women.

"People are not just subscribing because I'm so special," Vanessa told *Business Insider.* "It doesn't just happen. I sit there for hours writing line-by-line to keep my audience watching and to keep them hitting the like and subscribe buttons." With strategic and intentional planning, she followed the first four steps of the creator business development process to perfection, as broken down in Table 8.2.

Ideation	Vanessa experimented with what type of content she wanted to create and share, starting with trending topics before eventually settling on the goal of educating her audience.
Development	She decided to launch an entirely separate YouTube channel dedicated solely to finance education for women, successfully leveraging her background as a certified financial education instructor and former accountant.
Growth	After finding her creator-market fit, Vanessa continued to create content, releasing multiple videos every month. Her audience is 91 percent female, which aligns with the demographic she wants to target.
Commercialization	YouTube monetized her channel four months after launch. She now earns over twenty thousand dollars each month from ad revenue and plans to diversify her income streams by launching a paid membership service, partnering with brands, and releasing a YouTube course.

Table 8.2: Vanessa's creator business development process (steps one through four).

EXIT

For a business, an **exit** is a successful transition to the next stage. Exits for private corporations generally fall into four buckets:

1. **Liquidation**: when a business shuts down its operations and sells its assets.
2. **Acquisition**: when a business is sold to another.
3. **Merger**: when two businesses combine into one.
4. **Initial public offering (IPO)**: when a business's shares of stocks are sold to the public.

Similarly, for creators, I ask the question, "What does life beyond content look like?"

As creators become the more prominent brands of our future, one question that remains to be seen is what a creator-business exit looks like. Currently, I have rounded up these four primary models as natural exit strategies.[1]

MODEL 1: MOVE ON.

This is the most straightforward exit strategy. The creator may decide they have accomplished everything they set out to do as a creator and want to move on to other priorities in life or other career modes instead, so they go all-in during their time as a creator and sprint until they reach the finish line they had set for themselves. However, given the sprinting mentality, this model can quite easily result in burnout. Thus, extra precaution must be taken to maintain mental health and boundaries.

For former lifestyle and beauty YouTuber Joyce Hsieh (@joyce), creating content was everything to her—until it wasn't. For five years, she posted makeup tutorials and everyday life vlogs ("video blogs"). Joyce grew to over 150,000 subscribers at her peak, signing with a prominent influencer management agency to create content fulltime. In tandem, she ran a women's clothing e-commerce brand, tapping into her content audience for growth, and had generated over two million dollars in revenue by the time she entered college.

However, she felt she needed to take a step back toward the end. "The fire to create that specific type of content just wasn't there anymore," Joyce told me. "I realized I didn't fully enjoy doing it as a fulltime job, and I wanted to dedicate my time to other things. I wanted to open up the door to all these other opportunities I didn't know existed because

---

1   It should be noted they are not perfectly analogous with the exits of private corporations. Furthermore, it is possible for a creator to choose more than one form of exit model to follow.

I have done social media for a very long time." In the two years that have passed since her last video, Joyce has spent that time exploring other interests and career paths. While she does not regret her departure from her life as a fulltime lifestyle creator, she has always kept the avenue of content creation open if it fits with her future goals.

A prominent creator who followed this exit model is Kevin "KevJumba" Wu. One of YouTube's earliest stars, Kevin created vlogs that garnered over three hundred million views and claimed the honor of owning the third most subscribed channel on the platform in 2008. With his meteoric rise to fame, he competed on reality show *The Amazing Race* in 2010 and landed a lead role in a crime drama film executive produced by Martin Scorsese. By the time the movie had been released in 2014, however, Kevin had made his YouTube channel private and withdrawn from content creation. "I didn't see YouTube as my end goal," he told *The Hollywood Reporter* in 2017. Instead, he sought to focus his time on feature films and personal growth, returning to college and embracing spirituality. While Kevin has since restored all his YouTube videos to be publicly available again, he has left his days as a YouTube creator behind in pursuit of his other dreams.

MODEL 2: OUTGROW YOUR CONTENT TO BUILD A BRAND EMPIRE.

In the previous chapter, we heard the story of Michelle Phan. At her YouTube channel's peak, she mostly withdrew from the world of content creation to focus on her ventures Ipsy and EM Cosmetics. Similarly, we saw how Jimmy grew his MrBeast empire from the ground up in this chapter and now funnels his content revenue into philanthropic efforts. In this model, content is secondary to the creator's brand.

To achieve this, the creator must align their content with the industry they want to build an empire in and establish themselves as an expert or trendsetter there. Rather than creating content for the sole purpose of entertaining, informing, or inspiring, they leverage their content as marketing for their brand. The creator will set up a long-term, multi-year plan that likely will revolve around partnerships, investments, and/or acquisitions. Ultimately, the creator will outgrow their content, potentially leaving the world of content entirely, to focus on growing their brand empire.

MODEL 3: USE YOUR EXPERTISE TO INVEST IN OTHERS.
With the audience and expertise a creator has established over time, they are in an excellent position to become investors themselves. Twitch streamer Pokimane, who we met in Chapter 1, invested in a muscle therapy product. Charli D'Amelio, TikTok's most followed personality and a teen herself, made her first start-up investment in a teen banking app, according to *TechCrunch*. Both creators publicly announced their investment, bringing greater publicity and cementing the products' growth and reputation in the long run.

Jimmy has also chosen a nascent investment avenue: investing directly in creators. Partnering with creator banking start-up Creative Juice, which he had also personally invested in, he launched a funding initiative that invested 250,000 dollars in four YouTube creators in exchange for a cut of their earnings. In an interview with *The Information* in March of 2021, he stated the goal is to help rising YouTubers "pour gas on the fire" the way a business would, by raising a small stack of cash as they're growing rapidly. Just like how he expanded the possibilities of how a creator could be their own business, Jimmy believes all creators are high potential businesses.

Jonathan Chang, an investor who creates TikTok videos (@venturecapitalguy) about venture capital to an audience of over ten thousand, sees creator-led venture firms as another promising trend to watch. During our conversation, he pointed out "venture capital funds need to differentiate themselves other than 'hey, we can provide capital to you.'" While traditional firms like Andreessen Horowitz and Sequoia Capital are attractive to raise funding from because of their long-established history and connections, creator-led venture funds are unique because they "can provide an audience instantly" to a company's products.

We're beginning to see this in action already. TikTok stars Josh Richards (@joshrichards), Griffin Johnson (@imgriffinjohnson), and Noah Beck (@noahbeck) joined forces to establish Animal Capital, a fifteen-million-dollar venture fund that bills itself as "the first venture firm with access to 100+ million engaged consumers across the world" on its website. Vine and YouTube content creator Jake Paul co-founded two small venture funds to invest in start-ups. As told to *TechCrunch*'s Connie Loizos, he fully believes "[venture capitalists] and people in the business world understand more and more how to work" with creators and how to leverage the expertise and audience creators can bring to the companies they invest in.

MODEL 4: SHARE OWNERSHIP.
Sam Lessin, a general partner at Slow Ventures, has spent the last two decades contemplating how to invest in individuals rather than companies. In recent years, he realized creators are the ideal individuals to begin sharing ownership. "These creators really are operating like businesses with huge communities…but no one's financing them," he shared in our conversation.

"Influencers need to start treating themselves like real businesses and selling equity that represents a share of their complete, worldwide, perpetual earnings," Sam wrote in *The Information* in January 2021. "By selling real equity in themselves, influencers will have access to far more capital at much lower prices from investors."

At Slow Ventures, Sam manages the Creator Fund, which has funds set aside to invest directly in creators. For each creator, the fund invests 500,000 to 1.5 million dollars in exchange for 5 percent of a creator's future earnings. But these investors should not be limited to large venture capital funds. What if the investors could be any one of us? Owning a part of their favorite creators can build greater alignment and loyalty among fans. Social tokens, a type of cryptocurrency that allows creators to monetize themselves through digital ownership, enable just that, and we will learn more about them in Chapter 12.

Further down the line, we may witness a future where creators hold their own IPOs. While no independent creator has gone public yet, esports company FaZe Clan has announced its plans to IPO in 2022. Once it happens, it will become the world's first publicly traded esports organization on the market. Apparel brand and gaming organization 100 Thieves, whose creators includes popular streamers Valkyrae and CouRage, appears to also be on its way to an eventual public offering; the brand has raised over 100 million dollars in funding rounds and currently stands at a 460-million-dollar valuation, according to *Variety*. Seeing companies like FaZe Clan and 100 Thieves, both of whose prosperous growth have been so closely tied to creators and creator platforms, succeed gives hope to the promise of independent creators going public one day.

•••

As you begin your creation journey, it would be wise to strategize like a business and consider what exit model(s) you prefer. Regardless of how you exit, the impact and brand your content has created will always live on. "What creators set out to do is create a personal brand that has enough value that can stand up on its own even after the virality dies down," Joyce reflected. "The hardest part about being a creator is you *are* actually a business, where you *are* also the product."

So the questions therein lie with you: What product do you want to create? What business do you want to build? What brand do you want people to remember?

In the previous chapter, we saw how creators can leverage their community and platform to lead thriving entrepreneurial ventures. This chapter acknowledged the importance of recognizing the role creators inherently have as their own business. As the Creator Revolution continues to evolve and grow, a key component to watch and await is the historic rise of creators as the brands of our tomorrow.

Creators are disrupting traditional business models. They will be the most valuable businesses of the future.

CHAPTER 9

Creators as Representation

"I wasn't going to let my introduction to the world be one of a story that I think has been told many times."

—GINA RODRIGUEZ, ACTRESS AND PRODUCER

When Tyreek Davis started posting videos for fun on TikTok in late 2018, he never imagined he would become a beacon of representation for many.

An aspiring actor and filmmaker with over 2.4 million followers on TikTok and a significant presence on Instagram, Twitch, and YouTube as well, Tyreek has grown a substantial following from his videos standing in front of his camera, donning superhero suits. In some videos, he acts out scenes and scenarios as a superhero; in others, he educates his audience on the diversity and backgrounds of superheroes. Over the years, he has cosplayed superheroes like Miles Morales/Spiderman, Black Panther, Green Lantern, Captain America, and Naruto, often collaborating with other cosplay creators as well. His audience and reach have landed him opportunities working directly with Marvel Studios and DC Films.

The more videos he posted, the more he realized his cosplay videos weren't just entertaining his audience. They also had a genuine impact on people, especially the Black community, by seeing representation in superheroes and media.

Representation has long been an issue in Hollywood. An in-depth research study conducted by the University of Southern California discovered only 15.7 percent of nearly four thousand speaking roles in popular films released between 2007 and 2019 were Black. As shown in Figure 9.1, this percentage has only continued to decline among other underrepresented races and ethnicities.

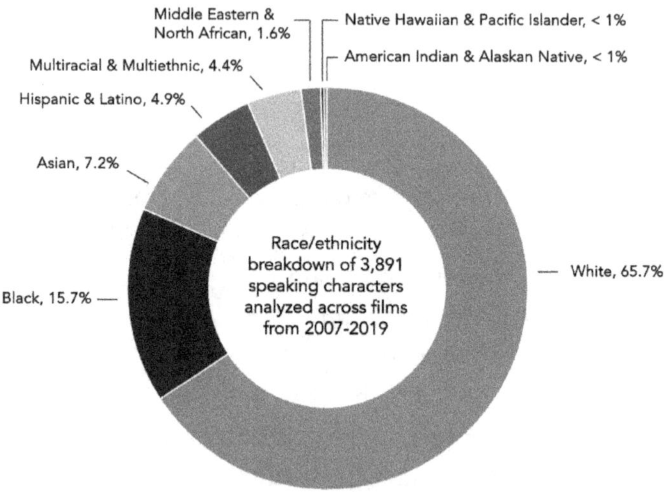

Figure 9.1: Race/ethnicity breakdown of 3,891 speaking characters analyzed across films from 2007 to 2019. All categories are labeled in accordance with the study's classifications. Data source: USC Annenberg, 2020.

"While traditional media has been slow to reflect the world we live in, the internet has opened the floodgates for diverse talent and stories," Index Ventures investor Rex Woodbury wrote in his newsletter *Digital Native.* "By removing the mostly-white, mostly-male gatekeepers of media, the internet ensured anyone could create content for audiences around the world."

Tyreek decided to embrace the burden that had been placed upon him and take the responsibility of creating impact and representation seriously. "All these people look up to me as a hero, because I represent [many different] superheroes… [They are] role models who represent a lot, especially toward the Black community as well," he said in our conversation. "I get to be that hero to others, so I represent something bigger than myself."

When fans recognize Tyreek and his cosplay friends on the street or at conventions, they get emotional seeing their superheroes in real life. In an art piece dedicated to Tyreek for his birthday, one Instagram fan wrote, "Thank [you] for just being [you]."

Tyreek has found a unique way to usher in Black representation in media—by cosplaying superheroes on social media. He is not the only creator who has recognized the unprecedented impact and power being a creator can have on representation. So far, Part II of this book has expanded upon how creators are revolutionizing themselves: creating their own opportunities, paving their own path to entrepreneurship, and establishing their individual selves as brands. In this chapter, we will add to that discussion by looking at another way creators are revolutionizing themselves: by amplifying representation for generations to come. Given the power of their voices, creators represent more than themselves. They are using their platforms to take the issue of imbalanced media representation into their own hands.

CREATION TO REPRESENTATION

It's hard to believe Jenna Wang once labeled herself a "super shy girl." Now a YouTuber with nearly 150,000 subscribers and over 12 million total views, Jenna is best known for her viral videos of dancing to K-pop (South Korean pop) songs in public settings such as tourist attractions and public high schools—not exactly the first thing that comes to mind for someone who is shy.

In high school, Jenna thought her future would entail being a doctor or lawyer—careers commonly associated (and stereotyped) with Asian Americans. Even though she dreamed of being a performer, Jenna never saw representation for Asian Americans beyond those two careers in her home state of Iowa.

"I couldn't really remember the last time I saw a movie or a show with actual representation... Same with political figures and journalists," she recalled to me. "They were mostly white, and that was the same way my school was—mostly white."

Everything changed when her friend showed her a K-pop video.

Suddenly, Jenna saw someone who looked like her performing. Not just performing—K-pop stars were revolutionizing the music industry with their stark fashion and blazing dance moves. The impact can still be seen today; by July of 2021, doing a quick search for "kpop in public challenge" gave me over eight hundred thousand videos on Google.

Captivated by the K-pop videos and tutorials she watched, she fell headfirst into the world of K-pop and dancing. In 2018, *Dance Magazine* remarked, "Today, choreography once considered sacred and only transferred person-to-person is now self-taught, edited, and remixed in bedrooms and basements." Jenna was one such dancer, using online tutorials to teach herself how to dance in the reflection of her bedroom's glass door.

With her newfound inspiration and skills, she began to dance spontaneously in public. Her sister filmed her dancing to South Korean boy band NCT U's song "BOSS" in front of The Bean, a prominent landmark in Chicago. She didn't care when tourists walked by or stopped to point at her; she just kept dancing. Then, she uploaded the video to YouTube, where many other dances found their home soon after.

Jenna's first million-view hit came months later. Wearing bright red lipstick, black boots, and an olive-colored jacket loosely tied around her waist, she danced to a popular K-pop star's dance cover of Jason Derulo's "SWALLA." She performed in an empty space in a dimly lit high school cafeteria, while students crowded around tables and walked in and out of the camera frame. She spun and strutted with graceful yet energetic dance moves, her two long braids swaying and swinging, beaming at the camera and completely ignoring the students cutting in front of and behind her.

Just as she had been inspired by Asian visibility on social media, she returned the favor to a new audience. Words of admiration from young Asian American women flooded the comments below her viral video. "She's breaking [A]sian stereotypes at an [A]merican high school!" one user wrote.

Now an undergraduate student, Jenna publishes videos on a less frequent basis. Despite this, she still occasionally gets recognized by college classmates for her dance videos. Jenna's journey from a super shy girl to becoming a viral YouTube dance sensation is a remarkable lesson on how the ease with which anyone can create and consume content is helping increase representation in media. The impact of content on representation worked in both directions: she was inspired by seeing videos she watched online, and her fans were inspired by seeing her content on YouTube.

As we discussed in Chapter 5, media consumption has traditionally been limited to the big screen, specifically movies and television. However, in the twenty-five years between *The Joy Luck Club* and *Crazy Rich Asians*, not a single big-budget Hollywood film with an all-Asian cast was released. The aforementioned University of Southern California study found thirty-six of the top hundred grossing movies in 2019 failed to depict even one Asian speaking or named character. To quote *Teen Vogue*'s Phillipe Thao, "a generation of Asian-Americans grew up with minimal mainstream representation."

Now, smaller screens—laptops, phones, and tablets—sit in front of us all the time. A research study conducted in 2019 found the average American spends 5.4 hours a day on their phone (Brown, 2019). With how easy it is to access these small screens, we have the ability to consume content with greater ease than movies and television shows.

With the Media Makeover and the growing prevalence of creator platforms and social media, many early creators paved the way to better Asian representation in the media, such as short film channels Wong Fu Productions (American) and JinnyboyTV (Malaysian); Lilly Singh, a Canadian comedian of Indian heritage with over fourteen million subscribers who had her own talk show on NBC; and Ryan Higa, an Okinawan-Hawaiian comedy creator who was once the most subscribed channel on YouTube for almost two years straight in the platform's early years. As an Asian American myself, these creators were instrumental in inspiring me to believe my ideas, writings, and art were worth sharing on the internet.

"I think it was so fresh and it was so strange for [fans] to see an Asian face, even though it wasn't on TV and it was just on a YouTube screen or a computer screen," Wong Fu Productions's Philip Wang said during an interview with *Insider* in 2021. "That was already such an impactful thing for them."

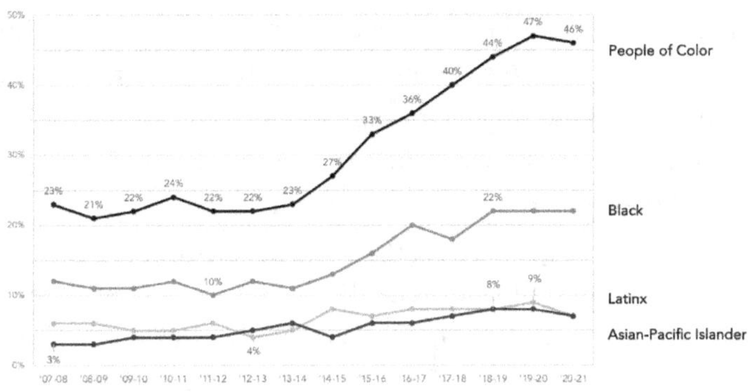

Figure 9.2: Graph documenting broadcast representation of TV series regulars over time. All categories are labeled in accordance with the study's classifications. Data source: GLAAD Media Institute.

For anthropologist Ren Fernández-Kim, finding representation that related to their identity on a screen was nearly impossible. Born to a Peruvian father and a Korean mother—"Koruvian," as Ren likes to say—they struggled to identify with both Latinx and Asian cultures growing up. "I grew up never quite loving both sides of me because I didn't fit in," Ren reminisced to *USA Today*. The lack of representation in media not only applied to both cultures separately, but also in an intersectional manner.

Recognizing the growing power of content, Ren decided to be the representation they sought as a child. So they began to publish infographics and videos on Instagram (@corpus-ren) educating others about Asian-Latinx culture, nonbinary and queer identity, anthropology, and personal stories. When *Shang-Chi and The Legend of The Ten Rings*, Marvel Studios's first film starring an Asian superhero lead, was set to hit theaters in 2021, Ren partnered with Disney to host an early screening for the Latinx and Asian communities. It included a pre-film discussion Ren prepared and workshopped with Disney, covering important topics such as the immigrant ideal, family, and representation.

Today, Ren has an audience of over twenty thousand following their journey. "We all have such a diverse story and diverse set of experiences. People might think 'oh, it's too small,' but no, that's not true. We're *all* out here and have important stories to tell," Ren emphasized in our conversation over the phone. "I am happy content creation and content platforms exist, because they give us an opportunity to kind of step into that power and make our own voices, make our own story."

With the rise of content creation comes a new era of creating representation in media. Tyreek, Jenna, and Ren, for example, may not have fully anticipated having this additional burden of representation when they first started creating content, but they have embraced their role and continue to strive for greater impact. They took issues of representation into their own hands and served as role models for future generations to look up to.

All that said, it is critical to also acknowledge the ease of content creation is by no means perfect: many of those at the top are still white and/or male.[2] *Forbes* found YouTube's top five highest-paid channels in 2021 consisted of MrBeast (54 million dollars), Jake Paul (45 million dollars), Markiplier (38 million dollars), Rhett and Link (30 million dollars), and Unspeakable (28.5 million dollars), all of whom are male and all but one are white. Chapter 11 details other forms of creator inequities as well. Change will not come overnight; we must collectively work toward addressing these inequities as a society. However, the Creator Revolution certainly has begun to enact impact and inspire, starting with one creator's presence at a time.

CULTURAL & IDENTITY AWARENESS

We have seen how creators can blaze trails by removing the gatekeeping of representation and voices in media. With over 355,000 followers on Instagram, Schuyler Bailar has shattered barriers and blazed trails in more than one way: as an athlete, as a creator, and as an educator.

Schuyler was a top-rated competitive swimmer throughout high school, setting a national relay record with future Olympic champion Katie Ledecky in 2013. He was recruited to swim for the women's team at Harvard University and had a bright athletic future ahead of him.

Then, after battling an eating disorder that forced him to delay his enrollment, Schuyler realized the eating disorder was merely a mask for an underlying gender identity issue: he was a transgender man. This was a massive revelation to reckon with, especially given the scarcity of transgender role models in the public eye at the time.

---

2   Any definition of "top" likely can apply here—most followed, highest earning, etc.

So he went online in search of any semblance of a transgender community and found one on Instagram. Schuyler then registered the account @pinkmantaray on Instagram. "I made my account completely anonymous because I didn't want anybody to find it," he recalled.

During that gap year before college, Schuyler underwent a double mastectomy and came to terms with his gender identity. To his relief, the university not only supported his transition, but also allowed him to swim for the men's team. With this decision, Schuyler became the first openly transgender swimmer in the history of National Collegiate Athletic Association (NCAA) Division I, the highest level of intercollegiate athletics in the United States (Mineo, 2019).

At the same time, he began to shift his use of Instagram. What began as a support community evolved into an outlet for storytelling and personal documentation. Schuyler posted about his transitioning journey, swim practices, and life at college. In 2017, a photo contrasting two before-and-after transitioning prom photos side by side turned viral, receiving over five thousand likes in one day. "This is unbelievably inspirational," one user commented on his post. "To have the courage to make such a huge change and to just be yourself without anyone's judgment stopping you…man…I'm just speechless. Incredible story to say the least, and you've definitely motivated and inspired me."

The reactions he received unveiled to him how social media could exist as an avenue to greater visibility of representation. "The most meaningful interactions I have on a pretty consistent basis, probably multiple times a week, [are] when I get a message. It's something along the lines of 'Hey, I read your posts, and it made me feel safe.' Or 'Hey, I'm really thankful I found you. Watching you be yourself has saved my life,'" Schuyler recounted to me. "I feel very privileged to be able to be in that position, and to be able to share openly about myself because it really does save lives. And it's not just because of me, it's just somebody answering their need for visibility that says '*hey, I'm here, you can be here too*'... I really want that to be a resounding message of my work."

Over time, he has become more deliberate about creating content that not only shares his journey as a transgender athlete, but also informs the public about queer resources and social justice issues. Rather than being referred to as a creator, Schuyler prefers to call himself "an educator who uses Instagram." He has published resources ranging from topics of transgender athletes to Asian American issues on his website and Instagram for individuals of any knowledge level to access. To avoid promoting or spreading any form of misinformation, he always conducts meticulous research and cites peer-reviewed sources in his posts.

While Schuyler recognizes the dangers of disinformation, after more than seven years of consistently creating and engaging on social media, he is also acutely aware of how influential content platforms have been to the queer community. "Social media has massively revolutionized accessibility to language and experiences that might reflect your own," he said. "I think more people are discovering they're queer sooner and with more ease, because we can see people online easily." We see this in action as the #lgbtq hashtag blooms in popularity every day, with over 20 million posts on Instagram adopting the hashtag. In comparison, according to nonprofit GLAAD's 2020 findings, queer characters appeared in only 18.6 percent (22 films) of 119 major movies released in 2019.

Access to broader representation has aided many individuals in better determining and learning about their identities.

Soon after downloading TikTok, twenty-year-old Kansas resident Riley came across the LGBTQ+ creator corner of the app. Riley watched videos released by non-binary creators like Adesso Laurenzo, James is Smiling, and Rain Dove and realized how much they related to these creators' stories and insights.

"Before I'd used the app, I hadn't heard of non-binary people. But after learning about this identity from non-binary creators, I was able to be like, 'Oh, wait! That's me! I'm non-binary,'" Riley told lifestyle publication *HelloGiggles*. "Truthfully, without it, I don't think I would have been able to come out."

Being able to hear a diverse array of perspectives allows for more nuanced visibility of people across spectrums of labels and identities, especially those who are less heard. In particular, Indigenous creators have used content platforms to raise awareness and dispel myths about their cultural traditions and histories.

A queer and transgender scholar born and raised within the Navajo Nation, Charlie Amáyá Scott was dissatisfied with online conversations they saw about Indigenous and queer representation. So they published long-form introspective essays and took to Twitter to share the pieces and more of their thoughts. "I wanted to reflect my experience, but also challenge the stereotypes people had," Charlie explained to me.

Over time, they joined TikTok and Instagram (@dineaesthetics) as additional channels to educate and raise awareness. Guided by their personal content mission statement of "inspiring joy and justice," Charlie showcases elements of their personal life and discusses Indigenous, transgender, and queer issues with their online communities. The

Reclaiming Native Truth study in 2018 found the inclusion of Indigenous characters in primetime television and popular films ranged from 0 to 0.4 percent; subsequent studies from the University of California Los Angeles showed Indigenous representation in film to be around 0.6 percent (Hawk, 2021). Given over 173,000 individuals follow Charlie across social media, we know people are interested in supporting authentic Indigenous voices and stories—we just need to provide them a platform to do so.

Despite already having a lot on their plate already as a PhD student, Charlie sees content creation as a critical mechanism for increasing representation and sharing faithful stories: "Social media, with the presence of Indigenous people doing amazing things and being authentic and real people—even just seeing us alive and existing and living—has really allowed representation to be more complex, more nuanced, and more in line with what contemporary understanding is starting to look like. Granted, yes, there are still some issues, but I would argue without content creation about social media, we would not be where we are today."

Simultaneously, we must acknowledge the burdens of increasing representation and education do not fall solely on the shoulders of creators from underrepresented groups. "Unfortunately, because [Indigenous creators] are such a small community, I think we become pigeonholed into being educators around all things related," Charlie reflected. Amplifying representation may begin with creators identifying with specific identities, but true representation relies on the rest of us to listen, learn, and showcase authentic stories going forward.

In her viral 2009 TED talk, Nigerian author Chimamanda Ngozi Adichie stated, "The single story creates stereotypes, and the problem with stereotypes is not they are untrue, but they are incomplete. They make one story become the only story." While traditional media has been slow to adapt to the ever-evolving world we live in and the plethora of stories it represents, content creation has enabled anyone to step up to the plate and share their stories. This has, in turn, augmented representation on social media and in traditional media, as well as increased cultural and identity awareness and education overall.

Part II of this book, "Self-Made Successes," has explored various paths creators are undertaking to revolutionize themselves. From blazing new trails to establishing business empires, creators play many important roles, but the role they hold as representation for many may just be the most impactful in the long run.

> Creators have the power to amplify representation.

PART III:

CHALLENGES AND OPPORTUNITIES

Parts I and II of this book have explored the largely positive impact creators generate for society and the new paths they can carve out for themselves. In Part III, "Challenges and Opportunities," we will delve into several major challenges creators face and suggest how they, and society as a whole, can work to address these issues.

Chapter 10 illuminates how being a creator provides a unique set of burdens and mental risks due to their online presence, especially pertaining to mental burnout, bullying, and harassment. It is critical for us to consider how we—as creators and consumers—can better confront and support these issues.

Chapter 11 introduces the concept of the creator middle class. The chapter then examines several inequities creators face and recommends potential solutions for them to weather these challenges.

Chapter 12 presents additional solutions to the challenges discussed in Chapter 10 and Chapter 11 from a futuristic perspective. While there certainly exists risk, lacking regulation, and undeveloped infrastructure, the emergence of blockchain-powered technologies enables new forms of content that could potentially reduce burnout and level the creator playing field.

The Dark Side

"There are two ways of spreading light: to be the candle or the mirror that reflects it."

—EDITH WHARTON, AUTHOR AND DESIGNER

When I first discovered the world of fanfiction, I began to write my own so I could immerse myself in the fictional universes I admired. I thought it would be a fun, harmless activity. After all, who would care that much about a twelve-year-old's writing, likely buried among millions of other stories on the internet?

It turned out, the answer was *a lot of people.*

I received death threats, negative reviews written in all-caps, and essay-length critiques in my inbox, some signed and some anonymous. The first time I received an aggressively rude review, I wanted to cry and stop writing altogether. Even today, I am still receiving these hateful comments on stories I published many years ago and haven't touched since. A reader recently left the profanity-laden comment, "Delete this f---ing garbage, and then delete your s----y f---ing profile from this website, you absolute f---ing inbred ape," in response to one story.

I knew hundreds of thousands of individuals read and appreciated my content. But that did not matter when the voices of the few—my critics and haters—rang the loudest and drowned out the rest. They made me constantly question myself. *Should I continue writing? Was I actually good enough to publish content online?*

In addition to the mental strain of fielding vitriolic comments, I struggled with the rapid pace I had not realized creators adhered to. My inbox was frequently flooded with comments such as "Where's your next chapter? I've waited a week already, and this is unacceptable." Keeping up with their demands was an impossible task. Writing was a slow, detailed process, and I couldn't keep up a schedule while still holding myself to the bar I set for my writing quality. Even the kindest comments served as a constant reminder that I needed to post *more* content *soon*—"I can't wait for your next piece!!", commenters flocked to write on my art posts. Forcing myself to pump out content on a tight timeline for the sake of my audience rather than myself crushed my spirit and turned a hobby into a chore. I still had to balance content creation with school, which proved to be far more demanding to keep up with than I had anticipated.

On top of it all, as a young and anonymous creator, I lived in fear of being "doxxed," which occurs when someone publishes your private or identifying information online. I watched several of my creator friends get doxxed by their haters, their full names and house addresses forever leaked on the internet without their consent.

I felt exhausted, frustrated, and pained. More than once I wanted to quit and erase every trace of my existence off social media. Finally, three years after I started my journey as a fiction and art creator, I stopped creating content and said goodbye to my online audience.

Unfortunately, I am not alone in these experiences.

In this chapter, we will take a deeper look at how being a creator provides a unique set of burdens and mental risks due to their online presence, especially pertaining to mental burnout, bullying, and harassment. It is critical for us to consider how we—as creators and consumers—can better confront and lend support to combat these issues.

BATTLING BURNOUT

When Nick Singh sits down at his desk every morning, he opens up LinkedIn and starts drafting a new post. After he publishes the post, he checks his notifications and replies to comments he received on his posts overnight. He spends the rest of the day responding to comments on his new post. At night, he checks the updated metrics of his post and his following. As he lies in bed, his mind churns through ideas for tomorrow's post.

Today, Nick has over 80,000 followers on LinkedIn and 46,000 newsletter subscribers who follow him for technology career resources and insights. In 2021, he co-authored and published the book *Ace the Data Science Interview*, which has since sold over 10,000 copies and become an Amazon bestseller in the data science genre. Despite his impressive accomplishments, he reflects on his content creation journey with some regrets.

During a hectic period in his personal and professional life, Nick went six months without posting on LinkedIn. Focusing on other things in life is a perfectly understandable reason to stop posting, but in hindsight, he regrets it.

"You know I [paused my posts] because I was focusing on other things, but let's be honest, I could have easily slept ten minutes less every single day and gotten something out there, right? Or in one hour—I could have found one hour on the weekend to do something, just one post even every week," he told me. He believes if he had maintained his consistency and growth trajectory, especially as an early creator on LinkedIn, he would have "ten times the audience" he currently has.

Many other creators echo Nick in the sentiment that consistency is one of the most important but challenging aspects of being a content creator. Lizzie Davey, an award-winning marketing writer, calls inconsistency the "biggest mistake" one can make in content creation. Not only has consistency been found to increase satisfaction and trust for consumers, but digital creators are forced to be consistent because platform algorithms prioritize creators who post content more frequently.

The fear of losing out to algorithms has frequently resulted in overworking and, eventually, **burnout** from the endless stream of creating content. Jack Innanen, a twenty-two-year-old TikTok star with over 2.5 million followers on the app, told *The New York Times*, "I feel like I can become washed up any second by an algorithm."

Content creation turns into an unending cycle:

- You post content.
- Your audience demands more content.
- You work to keep up until you burn out or slow down.
- Your audience starts to decline.
- You are under pressure and have to create more content.
- Repeat (until exit).

Despite having greater control and autonomy, there is no work-life balance for a creator if one wants to get ahead. It's hard to justify taking breaks when consistency and frequency are rewarded.

During a trip studying a house of influencers, *Harper's Magazine* writer Barrett Swanson recalled, "At one point, [one of the influencers] comes over and says, 'The scary thing is you never know how long this is going to last, and I think that's what eats a lot of us at night. It's like, what's next? How long can we entertain everyone for? How long before no one cares, and what if your life was worth nothing?'"

No one should ever feel their value or life's worth is dependent on a few numbers, but all too often creators feel like this is the case. Their content, discoverability, and revenue are directly tied to their audience size and engagement metrics, which are controlled by the platforms' opaque and constantly changing recommendation algorithms. As a result, many creators experience burnout.

The word "burnout" was first coined by American psychologist Herbert Freudenberger in the 1970s. He used the term to describe the effects of severe stress and high ideals in "helping" professions, such as doctors and nurses who would often "sacrifice themselves for others." Today, the usage of "burnout" refers to any type of prolonged stress, not just helping professions. Anyone, from overworked employees to overburdened homemakers, can experience burnout.

For creators, mental burnout can arise from a variety of factors:

- Frustration over stagnant audience growth.
- Stress over finances.
- Underperforming content and metrics.
- Struggling to come up with new content ideas (e.g., writer's block).
- Exhaustion from publishing content consistently.
- Challenge of balancing content creation with a fulltime job, family, etc.

- Impostor syndrome.
- Hate comments, cyberbullying, backlash, and more.

"I don't know a single creator who hasn't burned out after doing it for three to five years," Daniel Koss, founder of creator tool start-up Creable, told me. A former gaming creator in Switzerland with over 400,000 subscribers and 72 million views, Daniel published videos on YouTube prolifically from 2009 to 2015. He explained, "There is an expectation for creators to constantly be active and posting content. At the same time, they want you to always reinvent yourself and always be generating new, better content. But once you actually truly change your content, they don't want that—they want you to stick to what you're doing. So this endless back-and-forth will result in burnout."

A 2022 report released by creator tool start-up Vibely surveyed 150 creators with followings that range from 100,000 to over 5 million. The report revealed a staggering 90 percent of the creators polled had experienced burnout, and 71 percent had considered quitting social media entirely. In a society increasingly reliant on digital content, it is worrisome how social platforms' algorithms are filling creators with constant fear, worry, and regret when it comes to consistently churning out content. This setup is directly leading to burnout and deteriorating mental health.

The advent of social platforms, in particular, has resulted in a previously unseen type of burnout: persona burnout.

When third-year college student Grace Yeung landed her first product management internship, she felt anxious about entering a new career field she had no prior experience in. Never did she imagine she would one day be helping many others land fulltime jobs in the industry, let alone that it would happen less than a year later.

The COVID-19 pandemic struck months later in early 2020. According to the International Labour Organization, the pandemic and the resulting lockdowns caused 114 million people globally to lose their jobs in 2020. Grace witnessed that firsthand, seeing both friends and strangers on LinkedIn lose internship and fulltime job offers or be laid off left and right. Wanting to assist such people in their job search, she quickly made a LinkedIn post offering to answer any questions about product management and résumé reviews for anyone interested.

Grace's post received over 100 comments in one week, much to her surprise. Fueled by the interest, she began to publish more posts on LinkedIn, as well as longer, in-depth articles on Medium, offering advice about internship and job recruiting, career development, and product management. Within a few months, she gained 11,500 followers on LinkedIn, gathered over 30,000 reads on her Medium articles, and co-founded a community of over 10,000 aspiring product managers.

In her current job as a fulltime product manager, two years after her first internship in the field, Grace met a new product manager at her company who told her that her LinkedIn and Medium content had helped him prepare for and land the new job. Unlike Grace, this new product manager wasn't a new college graduate; instead, he had already worked in the industry for a few years but had wanted to change roles.

"Here was someone who has been in the industry for so long and yet found value in my pieces," she reflected. "[Content creation can] bring value to people in a scalable way."

Despite her sizable online audience and her acknowledgment of the value she's created in helping others in their career development, Grace had not posted on LinkedIn in over three months when I spoke with her. She wanted to reassess her content on the platform, because she didn't want people to view her solely based on her job title and company name.

"I want people to see me as a holistic individual outside of just the workplace, because I actually have hobbies and interests and fun experiences," she said. "I feel like LinkedIn is a place where I'm just primarily talking about my professional self, which I think is a big part of me, but that's not all of me. Creating content on that platform for so long has made me feel pigeonholed into that."

Grace is not the only creator who has struggled with their identity and authenticity online. *Vox* journalist Rebecca Jennings describes creators as having two identities they toggle between: "the real person" versus "the online persona." Many young individuals have even more identities to toggle among, creating multiple social media accounts to showcase different personas or parts of their lives (often on different platforms too).

I call this phenomenon **persona burnout**: when people burn out from needing to balance multiple personas and giving each persona their full energy and thought.

"Gen Zs are brand strategists from age ten. They learn: okay, my Instagram needs to be like this, my YouTube needs to be like this, my TikTok needs to be like this, my Twitter needs to be like this. It's so different than how Millennials and Gen X perceive content," Tiffany Zhong, founder of multiple creator tool start-ups, said on venture capital firm a16z's podcast.

An increasing number of youths have fake Instagrams, also known as "finstas," to present an authentic version of themselves to a close circle of friends. After studying creators for many years, journalist Taylor Lorenz agrees with Zhong's conclusion. "I think in each place you're a different type of authentic version of yourself. I think Snapchat, you go to chat and you post things on Snapchat you wouldn't post on your finsta, you post stuff on your finsta you wouldn't post on your main [Instagram]," she said to *The Verge.*

Even higher profile creators face these issues. One of the first musicians to leverage TikTok to catapult her music into global hit songs, pop superstar Olivia Rodrigo told *GQ* magazine, "Something I learned very early on is the importance of separating person versus persona. When people who don't know me are criticizing me, they're criticizing my persona, not my person. But that's really difficult, though, too, because my persona is being as genuine and honest as I possibly can, so it's this weird dichotomy."

The struggle between a creator's authentic self and their online personas will only continue to widen. The number of creators experiencing mental burnout, including persona burnout, will continue to rise, which will negatively affect the impact creators could generate for society. To improve this, creators will need to move away from a reliance on platform-owned content and audiences (which we will read more about in Chapters 11 and 12) and instead toward more viable mechanisms of content creation that do not so easily lead to burnout.

When I asked Jade Darmawangsa, YouTuber and founder of influencer marketing agency X8 Media, where she sees the future of the Creator Revolution going, she said, "I think creators are going to slow down, take time off, and spend time on their mental health. There are going to be more ways for creators to have a sustainable business." With the conversation around mental health issues for creators more amplified and visible today, she is confident that "everyone will find a way to find a more sustainable way to make content."

Burnout can affect any creator, regardless of their audience or content niche. It is essential to embrace the journey, focus on the impact, and prioritize yourself as you determine what works best for you.

CREATOR TIP:

How do I overcome burnout?

Burnout can manifest through physical symptoms (gastrointestinal distress, insomnia, muscle pain, etc.) and emotional symptoms (apathy, anxiety, depressions, detachment, etc.). If you recognize any symptoms, you may be suffering from burnout.

Here are a few suggestions on how to handle burnout:

- **Schedule breaks.**
  Having pockets of time to recharge yourself is necessary for preventing mental fatigue. Yes, taking breaks is not ideal for content frequency, but your mental health is far more important in the long run than a small uptick in numbers. If you are concerned about your content schedule, you can queue content to publish during a longer break. Remember everyone has a different preference for recuperation and recharging, so consider what is the best schedule and mechanism for you.

- **Separate your person from your persona.**
  Creating digital content is a taxing experience, so it is
  critical to separate your online identity from your real-
  life presence. Taking breaks will also aid in reinforcing
  the separation. Ask yourself, what kind of separation
  do you want to create? Remember when haters criticize
  your content, they are attacking your persona, not your
  person.

- **Focus on impact, not numbers.**
  This is far easier said than done, but it is critical to
  recognize not every piece of content will do well and
  explode in popularity. Consider your favorite musician; they, too, must experience a significant difference
  between their hit songs and their less popular songs.
  Do not base your worth as a creator on metrics; instead,
  concentrate on the value you have provided and can
  continue to deliver.

- **Consider more scalable forms of content and income.**
  Monetization strategies such as developing an online
  course or building a membership community are more
  scalable and can generate additional passive income. In
  Chapter 12, we will also discuss newer forms of content
  powered by blockchain technologies that seek to make
  content creation more sustainable.

- **Seek professional help.**
  Many creators I interviewed for this book openly discussed their experiences with therapy. Processing your
  inner feelings can be cathartic and insightful, so it may
  benefit to observe and analyze your experience from an
  outside perspective. If you experience serious physical
  symptoms, please consider visiting a physician as well.

HANDLING HATE AND PARASOCIAL RELATIONSHIPS

Cameryn Grace Hodges was a massive fan of creators who recorded their day-to-day lives. As she entered high school, she thought it would be fun to document her high school journey on YouTube so she could look back at those moments in the future, just like her favorite vloggers (video bloggers). From her summer travels to winter morning routines, she filmed the little moments in her life she wanted to share with her audience.

What her favorite vloggers did not prepare her for were the reactions she would get. Immediately after she started her YouTube channel, she was bullied so often her high school classmates pushed her to tears nearly every week. No one else in her school created on YouTube at the time, so publishing content online made her the odd one out. To them, "being creative was weird," Cameryn recalled to me.

Many popular creators have become more transparent about their bullying experiences in recent years. Now the most-followed Minecraft streamer on Twitch, Thomas "TommyInnit" Simons created his first YouTube channel around the age of twelve. But he stopped uploading to that channel after he "was bullied about it at school," as he revealed in an interview with fellow YouTube star Anthony Padilla. Beauty and lifestyle influencer Eva Gutowski, with over 30 million followers across her social media, told *Teen Vogue* that trolls would target just about anything she posted: "Literally you could post anything and someone will always have an opinion, whether it's positive or negative."

According to the Cyberbullying Research Center, 73 percent of students had been bullied at school and 34 percent of students had experienced cyberbullying in their lifetime. The evolution of the internet, with social media making space

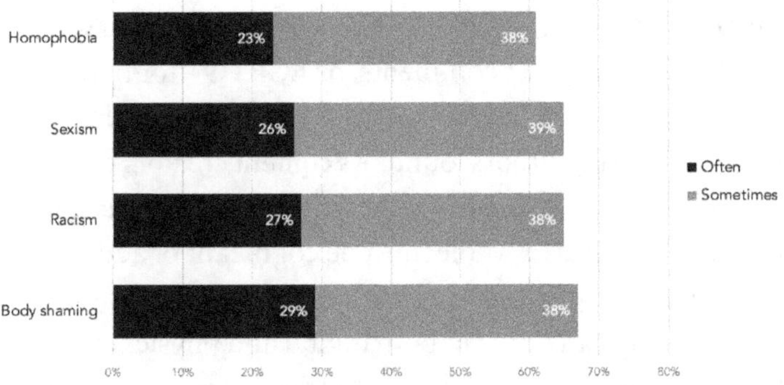

Figure 10.1: Out of 1,442 social media users of age 14 to 22 surveyed, this is how often they encountered different categories of hate speech on social media. Data Source: Rideout et al., 2021.

for the growth of content creators, has also given way to new reasons for bullying and ease of access for cyberbullying. When I walk down the street, strangers don't hurl insults and profanities at me every day, but I do receive them in my inbox when I sit behind my computer. When you feel like just one of uncountably many internet users and can hide behind a veil of anonymity, it is much easier for anyone to write aggressive attacks and comments. In an interview with *Teen Vogue*'s Sam Dolph, LGBTQ+ advocate and YouTube creator Shannon Beveridge advised other creators to "[not] acknowledge [the bullies] because if you do, you give their words power."

With how prevalent digital content is today, new content creators will likely face more bullying than they have ever experienced in the early days of online content, both in-person and online, for putting themselves out there. A study on how fourteen- to twenty-two-year-olds engage with social media found around one quarter of them say they "often" encounter body shaming (29 percent), racist (27 percent), sexist (26 percent), or homophobic (23 percent) comments on social media (Rideout et al., 2021). "Those in the targeted groups (e.g., Blacks for racist comments, or LGBTQ+ for homophobic ones) are more likely than others to be exposed to such comments," the authors found. As content creators continue to grow younger, this is a concern these social platforms and our society as a whole must be cognizant of addressing.

As we saw for the aforementioned creators, harassment and bullying can occur in both digital and physical settings. When harmful actions are taken to an extreme, however, they can permanently alter and even endanger the lives of creators.

A former interior designer, Blaire livestreams a variety of content that spans video games and cake baking under the online alias "QTCinderella," and has over 706,000 followers and 8.5 million watch hours on Twitch. Over time, she noticed an increasing number of men treated her as their "online girlfriend," despite none of them knowing her personally. They acted like they knew her well and expected her to lavish them with individual attention and affection. In 2020, she discovered a terrifying Reddit forum dedicated to "supposedly erotic images from her livestreams, such as a screenshot zoomed in on her butt that showed her bending over in her kitchen while putting cookies in the oven, looping GIFs of Blaire sitting up and back down to simulate a sexual motion, and links to Discord and Telegram channels containing far worse," as documented by *The Huffington Post*.

When the author of the article complained to Reddit about the incident, Reddit banned the subreddit harassing Blaire, citing "excessive copyright removals." A new subreddit was established almost immediately and remains active to this day.

Blaire thus turned to an online content removal firm to attempt to take down the photos of her that she never agreed to being posted online, which charged her 2,500 dollars a month. "My only option is to pay to get these taken pictures down or just find a different job," she said in the interview. "I think about that all the time."

CREATOR TIP:
Important Resources

- **National Suicide Prevention Lifeline**
  A United States-based suicide prevention network that provides free, 24/7, and confidential support to anyone in suicidal crisis or emotional distress.
  Phone: 1-800-273-8255
  Website: suicidepreventionlifeline.org
- **Crisis Text Line**
  Free, 24/7, and confidential mental health texting service available in the United States, Canada, United Kingdom, and Ireland.
  Website: crisistextline.org
- **Befrienders Worldwide**
  A global volunteer-run mental health network with 349 emotional support centers in 32 countries.
  Website: befrienders.org
- **The Trevor Project**
  Free, 24/7, and confidential crisis support services to LGBTQ+ young people.
  Phone: 1-866-488-7386
  Messaging: Text START to 678-678
  Website: thetrevorproject.org
- **More International Resources**
  unitedgmh.org/mental-health-support
  checkpointorg.com/global

In 1956, decades before the internet even existed, sociologists Richard Wohl and Donald Horton coined the concept of **parasocial relationships** to explain how audiences developed long-term attachments to high-profile media figures based on what they learned or "knew" about the figure. Even though relationships are generally bidirectional, parasocial relationships consist of one-sided affection: a fan gets attached to a celebrity, invests emotional energy and time, and feels as though they know the media figure personally, while the celebrity is completely unaware of the individual fan's existence.

"The audience actually has an active role in the content that is created," said Arienne Ferchaud, an assistant professor in the School of Communication at Florida State University, in a conversation with *The Verge*. "It sort of blurs the line between creator and viewer [in a way] that hasn't been possible before."

Nowadays, the advent of creator platforms, which can foster direct interaction between the creator and consumer, has augmented the dangers of parasocial relationships. "The personalities we see on screen, they're speaking to us directly," said Glenn Cummins, an associate professor of journalism and creative media industries at Texas Tech University (Skinner, 2020). "In contrast with a character we might see on a fictional TV show, we feel like we know them because we've seen them so much, but they're not really talking to us directly."

This phenomenon has led to fans engaging in outrageous behavior, such as harassing female streamers like Blaire or stalking and showing up to creators' houses uninvited. A thirty-year-old man was arrested for trespassing on then-eighteen-year-old YouTuber James Neese's house

(Istein, 2017). Early YouTube star Ryan Higa revealed on the *OfflineTV Podcast* that fans still visit his childhood home despite him living many states away now. On the violent extreme end of the spectrum, YouTube singer and songwriter Christina Grimmie was fatally shot by an obsessive fan who spent most of his waking hours watching her videos (Dendy, 2016).

The rippling dangers of harassment are amplified because creators have both a digital and physical presence, leaving neither their online nor everyday lives safe from hate and unwanted interactions. The effects on their mental well-being can be devastating, and some creators eventually stop creating content altogether as they experience burnout from a passion they once loved.

Figure 10.2: Compared to older generations, Generation Z (individuals born between 1997 and 2012) are the least likely to report very good or excellent mental health states. Data source: American Psychological Association, 2018.

As a creator again today, I publish content on Twitter, LinkedIn, and Substack. But now that I've been through the ebbs and flows of content creation before, I'm approaching it very differently this time. I mute or ignore comments regularly, reminding myself they are criticisms of my content, not of myself. I use my real name, so I no longer need to mentally tiptoe around every sliver of content I publish, wondering if it would expose my identity in any manner, but I am still careful about what I choose to disclose on the internet. To avoid burnout, I approach my growth with a more forgiving attitude and make room for recovery.

Creating content with the added elements of stress, burnout, cyberbullying, harassment, etc. will only exacerbate the mental health risks across all generations, particularly Generation Z, who are the least likely generation to report positive states of mental health, according to the American Psychological Association. This is an imperative social issue that must be addressed. We will need stronger community-based responses and solutions of support. We will need more forms of education (including online content) that promote mental-health literacy, including highlighting symptoms of stress and burnout as well as publicizing the resources of intervention and help. We will need to establish alternative paths for creators that are more sustainable for their mental well-being and build functionalities to support their physical, mental, and emotional needs.

To help mitigate these issues and build a brighter future of the Creator Revolution, we—creator platforms, creator tools, creators, consumers, and society as a whole—all need to consider these issues at a deeper level and invest in more support for creators.

> Being a creator carries undue burdens, particularly the development of mental burnout, online hate and harassment, and parasocial relationships.

CHAPTER 11

The Hidden Class

*"A journey of a thousand miles
must begin with a single step."*

—LAO TZU, PHILOSOPHER AND WRITER

During the day, Kacie Iuvara teaches creative arts subjects to elementary and middle school students. In the evenings, however, she leaves the world of teaching and steps into the shoes of a creator. Hunched over her desk late at night, she tirelessly works on multiple projects at the same time: a middle-grade fantasy book, three podcasts, and a webtoon (a form of digital comic).

Kacie has considered herself a creative her entire life. She finished her first full-length novel at the age of thirteen. "It wasn't good, but it was completed," she said to me with a laugh. More than a decade later, she is still creating content, but in a different manner—all of her content now lies on the internet.

Despite the fact she has been publishing online for over two years, she still finds earning money from content to be a difficult task. While making money is not her primary content creation goal, she still believes it is critical that content creation can become a self-sustaining business. "To balance making money and making art…at the beginning, it felt impossible," Kacie mused.

At the start of a creator's journey, one often lacks the funds, resources, time, knowledge, and connections to take off. Nevertheless, they—like everyone else—must still compete with the top creators.

Creating online content presents its own set of logistical challenges. Kacie enjoys the moments when she is recording her podcasts, drawing comic illustrations, and composing music for new podcast episodes. But she often feels set back by the elements beyond direct artistic creation that are equally, if not more, important, such as self-promotion, podcast editing, and audience building. For an amateur podcaster like herself, even finding the best online podcast hosting service was a challenge and took a lot of time to research and verify. That time is valuable time that other creators with more professional or prepared backgrounds are using to surge ahead and leave new creators in the dust.

Being a fulltime creator or "hustler" is extremely difficult to succeed at and "requires so much emotional investment and time," which is a luxury not many individuals have, as prominent internet culture journalist Taylor Lorenz said on *Means of Creation*. For example, the majority of Substack's paid newsletter writers are white men who have worked in industries like technology, business, or politics (Fischer, 2020). They often come from a place of comfort where they can leave their fulltime roles at companies or media organizations, likely giving up a regular salary and health insurance, to carve their own path.

While the now-social nature of the internet has eliminated many barriers for any creator to start and flourish, creators do not all begin at an equal starting line. As passion economy pioneer Li Ji pointedly stated, "The creator economy needs a **middle class**." In other words, so much focus is placed on the top tier of creators without enough support for aspiring, new, and smaller creators.

When we inspect the direct payouts creators receive on different platforms, we notice a tiny percentage of creators reap an overwhelming majority of rewards.

- In 2020, the top 1.4 percent of Spotify's musical artists earned 90 percent of total royalties, earning an average of 22,395 dollars per quarter each. The remaining 98.6 percent of artists, numbering over 3 million, earned only 36 dollars per quarter each (Ingham, 2020).
- The top 1 percent of streamers on Twitch earned more than 50 percent of all revenue on the platform, which has nearly 5 million creators. According to *The Wall Street Journal*, over 75 percent of Twitch streamers earned less than 120 dollars in the first ten months of 2021.
- The top 1 percent of Gumroad's 46,000 creators received roughly 60 percent of the money distributed in 2020. The top 10 percent of creators received nearly 92 percent of all funds.
- Substack announced in 2021 its top 10 publications earned more than 20 million dollars per year. Smaller newsletter writers, on the other hand, struggle to earn even hundreds of dollars.
- In 2021, *Axios* discovered the top 1 percent of podcasts receive 99 percent of all downloads.

This phenomenon is not new. In traditional news journalism, we have seen large publications like *The Wall Street Journal* or *The New York Times* attract millions of digital subscribers, while small, regional publications suffer layoffs and declining subscriptions despite offering a niche and differentiated product. Internet theorist Clay Shirky coined this phenomenon as the "power law distribution," which states that in a world with so much freedom to choose among many options (in this case, options of content to consume and creators to consume from), a small subset of the options will receive a disproportionate amount of attention or income even if this was not an intended outcome of the system.

However, this 90/10—or, even more drastically, 99/1—disparity still far overshoots the commonly assumed 80/20 distribution. Unequal access to education, time, and financial resources is certainly a contributor to this disparity. The ultimate root cause, however, is the engine of content success: recommendation algorithms.

In the previous chapter, we saw how opaque platform algorithms contributed to creator burnout. Contrary to the creative spirit, creator platforms seek to reward popularity and engagement over content quality and originality. As a result, smaller creators are drowned out by the tides of already popular creators who pander to the algorithms, struggling to get noticed by new audience members. In other words, the creator middle class has become hidden—hidden by the platform algorithms that are supposed to help these creators get noticed.

This chapter, in addition to the discussion of inequities present toward creators, will address the remedies and provide concrete recommendations to creators on how to work toward addressing these inequities. Ultimately, we as a society must band together to address these issues and work toward a more equitable stake for all contributors of the Creator Revolution.

COMMUNITY SUPPORT AND FEEDBACK

Cracking the code to content algorithms has long been a shared goal among creators. The logic went as follows: creators want to grow but don't know what the algorithm likes; on top of its lack of transparency, the algorithm is likely constantly evolving. Creators should strive to overcome the "impossible" will of the algorithm by remembering interactions and engagement always feed the algorithm in the meantime.

The most effective strategy for increasing interactions and engagement is to cultivate a loyal community and capitalize on your superfans.

A product manager at Cameo, a marketplace that connects superfans with their favorite stars and creators, Shreya Sudarshana spends her days brainstorming how to best build the future of fan experiences. "Realistically, creators need a community in order to be successful. That means success equates to asking: are you able to find a community in which you are able to drive engagement, retention, and everything in between?" she pointed out to me.

Content production is unidirectional, in which the creator pushes out content to their audience. Community development, on the other hand, is a closed loop. It is a deliberate process that involves back-and-forth conversation not only between a creator and their fans, but also within the fan base itself.

This was a lesson that Rosie Nguyen learned firsthand. As she struggled to put herself through four years of university, a burden compounded by taking care of a disabled parent, Rosie openly discussed her financial challenges on Twitter. Much to her surprise, strangers did not just send her generous words of support; some also sent her money.

"The internet is a place where people care about other people first, right?" she reflected in an interview with *Bustle*.

On Twitter, Rosie—who takes the online pseudonym Jasmine Rice (@jasminericegirl)—also learned about OnlyFans, a digital platform where creators charge their viewers to see their photos and videos.[3] She signed up for the platform to test it out. Within a few months, she had "made more than [her] family has ever made in a year."

While creating content on OnlyFans, Rosie saw how much people craved personal and candid connections and valued a close-knit community. Her creator experience, however, was marred by harassment, trolls, and consistently unpleasant attitudes of entitlement from the OnlyFans audience.

Inspired by her learnings, she decided to build a better solution and co-founded the creator platform Fanhouse. "Connect directly with your fans and earn money by growing your exclusive, authentic community," the app's homepage beckons today. Fanhouse encourages creators to grow their community even with as few as twenty followers, because the team understands how impactful community support is to every level of creator. "There's pride in the community around supporting a creator who everyone loves," Rosie told *Digital Native*.

Thus, it is critical for any creator, no matter how big or small, to carefully cultivate a close-knit community. Seek out audience input and feedback on a regular basis, then listen to what content they want to see more of in the future. This is not limited to simply reading the comments one receives. For example, Outschool, a marketplace of virtual classes for

---

3   OnlyFans's lack of content restrictions has led to the platform being most commonly associated with graphic and not-safe-for-work content, but that is not the only type of content on the site.

children, gathers parents' requests for future class topics and sends teachers a weekly email highlighting these requests. As mentioned in Chapter 5, Casey Newton—a former journalist turned independent writer—runs a Discord server where his paid subscribers can submit interesting topics for him to write about, meet each other, and discuss his newsletter content. Gathering feedback helps creators understand what niches their audience is most interested in, and if the audience is satisfied, they will engage more going forward, thereby propelling the community loop forward.

Following the metric of success Shreya proposed, it is essential to consider all pockets of the internet. Who are all the potential fans you can and want to target? How do you build the community so its experience is the best it can be both for you and your fans? As you navigate the inherent challenges and inequities of creator platforms, capitalizing on community in creative ways would be a helpful place to start.

EDUCATION AND TRAINING

Since its inception in 2005, YouTube has taken off as a global vehicle for content creation and expression. Video content uploaded by women-led channels in the Middle East and North Africa has seen a year-to-year growth of 50 percent. Saudi Arabia, in particular, had the highest YouTube watch time per capita around the world, and videos created by many of the top female Saudi YouTubers were found to be five times more engaging than the average YouTube video (Marshall, 2016).

However, many creators and fans are unaware of how the creation experience is not the same for everyone. For instance, cultural norms may influence or be a barrier to the content produced. Many of the current top female YouTubers across the Middle East and North Africa, including Asrar Arif (over 1.3 million subscribers, 146 million views), Amal Elmziryahi (over 662,000 subscribers, 97 million views), Hessa Al Awad / "Miva Flowers" (over 585,000 subscribers, 80 million views), and Al Juhara Sajer / "JaySajer" (over 512,000 subscribers, 55 million views), all began creating videos that only featured their hands. They did not dare to show their face, body, or personality on camera at the time due to cultural norms and expectations.

In her early videos, Amal used an overhead camera to film herself painting ceramic roses, baking beautiful desserts, and cooking Middle Eastern dishes. Her face did not appear in a video thumbnail until six years into her YouTube career. Similarly, Hessa began posting videos ten years ago, exclusively performing manicures and only showing her fingers and nails; today, her face appears in almost every video and thumbnail.

YouTube's employees only discovered this cultural barrier after speaking with these creators. Then, they worked closely with them to brainstorm and optimize content with these limitations in mind. YouTube generally advised you to put your face as prominently in videos and thumbnails as possible; here were examples of creators who could not follow this educational tip. Because of the high variability that comes with being a creator, it would be impossible to write a singular playbook on how to succeed as a creator.

This is where creator platforms and tools can come in to help. The first step is to offer direct assistance to up-and-coming creators in the form of education, training, and more tailored support.

To help make content creation more accessible to a wider range of creators, content platforms need to spend time helping and educating creators on how to best grow and scale.

When growing the YouTube creator presence in emerging markets, the platform's Creator and Artist Partnerships team dedicated a lot of their time to educating creators. They taught in-person workshops for high-potential creators, which helped creators connect with one another. They also established the Creator Academy and launched the NextUp contest, two larger initiatives designed to help YouTube creators elevate their content and grow their audience.

In China, influencer incubators have propagated and developed a multi-step process to identify, grow, and monetize creators, which they also refer to as key opinion leaders (KOLs). One such business, Ruhnn, went public in 2019 after its hundreds of contracted KOLs generated 2 billion RMB (300 million USD) in total sales. The first influencer they signed was fashion blogger Zhang Dayi. Two years later, her store aggregated 46 million dollars in revenue sales in 2016, which was more than Kim Kardashian's earnings of 45.5 million dollars that year (Wu, 2017).

The type of education and support provided by creator platforms should also keep cultural and societal barriers in mind. In the same way Middle Eastern and North African female YouTube creators demonstrated how the existence of cultural norms influenced their content presentation, societal structures and customs lead to inequitable problems that platforms need to be mindful of.

On TikTok, many Black creators felt the app's algorithm gave them less visibility and more stringent scrutiny of moderation rules. Visibility and moderation are tied directly to sponsorship and opportunities, so more views and fewer suspended videos equate to better experiences as a creator. In 2019, fourteen-year-old Jalaiah Harmon choreographed and posted a dance on Instagram. Known as the Renegade, the dance quickly blew up and became a viral sensation when it was brought to TikTok by another user. TikTok's biggest creators, including its most followed user, Charli D'Amelio, all followed suit and performed the dance. But credit became attributed to Charli, not Jalaiah. When visibility equates to income, a platform that unintentionally limits the visibility and reach of creators of color can harm the opportunities of many (Asare, 2020). When considering how to improve education and support for emerging creators, platforms need to pay close attention to these issues and barriers.

While content platforms can greatly help democratize access and resources for creators, building an equitable ecosystem for digital creators will take time. Society's own evolution toward eliminating barriers over time will also play a role. As much as their team had worked on combating the issue, the industry is "not totally democratized, and I don't think that is something platforms can solve alone—it's also a function of society," Jad Esber, a former member of YouTube's Creator and Artist Partnerships team, reflected in our conversation.

Inversely, creators should actively seek out opportunities for education, training, and capital. To meet this demand, more platform-targeted and niche-specific resources, incubators, and training programs are being launched. In the last two years, for example, the following programs have emerged:

- Google launched the "Google for Creators" resource in 2021 to help creators grow and get content inspiration.
- Substack introduced a two-month mentorship program, Substack Bridge, that pairs new and veteran writers to reach writing goals and grow on the platform.
- LinkedIn launched a 25 million dollar creator fund in 2021 for aspiring creators on the platform to participate

in a network, access new features, and receive a 15,000 dollar grant.

- Pinterest began to institute regular cohorts of their creator fund, which offered four weeks of hands-on training workshops, personalized consulting, and 25,000 dollar grants to empower underrepresented creators.

As we discussed in greater depth in Chapter 7, a platform's educational resources and workshops are an important investment in creators. Creator platforms want to help magnify the reach and success of every creator, so taking advantage of their resources, training, and capital is another possible path toward greater success as a rising creator.

CREATOR COLLABORATION

OfflineTV was formed in 2017 by a group of content creators who wanted to create videos together. "I wanted to live with people and make cool stuff with other people," OfflineTV founder and Twitch streamer William "Scarra" Li told esports publication *Inven Global*.

The creators each had their own content and revenue streams already. By living and working together, they could collaborate and create even more content, boosting all of their content presences collectively. Today, OfflineTV consists of eight creators: Scarra, musician Lily "LilyPichu" Ki, comedy engineering YouTuber Michael Reeves, and streamers Jeremy "DisguisedToast" Wang, "Sydeon," "QuarterJade," "Masayoshi," and Imane "Pokimane" Anys, whom we met in Chapter 1 (Garcia, 2021). Their content collective's YouTube channel has over 3 million subscribers and has amassed over 480 million views, demonstrating the advantages of capitalizing on a diverse range of content and audiences.

OfflineTV is not the only content group who has discovered collaborations are extremely valuable. In 2014, a group of YouTube creators formed the collaboration channel Our Second Life and lived together in the "02L Mansion." Many of Vine's eventual biggest stars, including Andrew "KingBach" Bachelor, Lele Pons, and Juanpa Zurita, lived in one large apartment complex in Los Angeles. In 2020, nineteen TikTok creators lived together in the Hype House. Its residents included the aforementioned Charli D'Amelio, who credits the house for expanding her creative and content horizons. "I'm trying things outside my comfort zone I might not have done if I was alone in my room," she told *The New York Times* in early 2020.

These content houses or collectives have proven to be extremely beneficial in accelerating audience growth. Collaborations can also take the form of establishing merchandise lines together, like how YouTubers Jeffree Star and Shane Dawson partnered for a year to create a docu-series about their upcoming makeup line. When their makeup finally went on sale, their flagship product—an eyeshadow palette—sold out in minutes. Earlier this year, creators J.J. "KSI" Olatunji and Logan Paul partnered to launch electrolyte drink brand Prime Hydration. According to *The Publish Press*, their Instagram Live announcement drew an eye-popping 540,000 fans in to learn more. Both collaborations demonstrated the power of two influencers bringing their audiences together.

When I was a new creator on Tumblr, my largest growth spikes came from collaborating with others. I worked together with some of my favorite fiction creators, which not only improved the quality of our art and writing pieces given our exchanged feedback, but also introduced our audiences to each other. In one Discord server, we organized an anthology of fiction pieces that turned into a successful charity fundraising effort.

Overall, creator collaborations can foster more creative ideas, joint content and ventures, and emotional support. These connections and collaborations can be so valuable to a rising creator's growth and success, so I hope to see platforms facilitate them more in the future. Similarly, creators should look for opportunities to collaborate with other creators and support each other's endeavors.

● ● ●

Serena Li Here lived in the San Francisco Bay Area, a prime location for learning about business models and technology. She spent two years as a product manager and product marketer at a medium-size, venture-backed start-up, and had worked at Merrill Lynch prior. Most importantly, she had been a devoted YouTube viewer for over ten years, forming real-life friendships with many YouTube creators.

So she thought to herself—how hard could it be to make money as a YouTube creator?

Serena quit her job at the start-up in 2020 to test out and research how hard it was to start a creator journey from scratch. She quickly learned the answer to her question was "a lot more difficult than what people are saying."

Despite all of the hype surrounding content creators, she realized growing as a creator was much harder than she anticipated. "If you started from scratch, and continued posting and exploring and iterating stuff from scratch with no track record, with absolutely no idea what to do to even become successful in a field, with no information and no network, it's quite difficult," she shared in our conversation. Despite living in the San Francisco Bay Area, where she had so much access to resources of understanding business models and monetization, she found the barrier to growth as a creator extremely hard to bypass.

Without a large enough audience, monetization wasn't even able to be in the equation. So how was a brand-new creator supposed to make money?

Serena expressed her concern: "If audience growth and content distribution for lower-middle class creators are not solved, these creators will not monetize. If everyone only pays attention to large creators and creator monetization, but they don't build enough framework to support the growth of smaller creators, the world will run out of creators."

To prevent this from happening, platforms need to recognize the inequities creators face and improve the experience to better support them. In an essay published in the *Harvard Business Review*, Li proposed ten strategies for content platforms to better democratize opportunities for creators to succeed:

1. Focus on content types with lower replay value.
2. Serve heterogeneity in user preferences and empower niches.
3. Recommend content algorithmically with an element of randomness.
4. Facilitate collabs and community.
5. Provide capital investment to up-and-coming creators.
6. Decouple creator payouts from audience demographic.
7. Allow creators to capitalize on superfans.
8. Create passive (or almost-passive) income opportunities for creators.

9. Offer a form of Universal Creative Income (i.e. provide creators with a basic income in order to incentivize more creators to devote more time to content creation).
10. Provide creator education and training.

In the meantime, creators can overcome these obstacles by capitalizing on communities and superfans, seeking educational resources and capital, and collaborating with other creators.

The Creator Revolution, and by extension our broader society, flourishes when every creator has an equal access to upward mobility and financial security. As we will see more of in the next chapter, it is up to us to build toward this vision.

> Creator platforms have skewed the creator landscape and bestowed most rewards toward the top 1 percent. To address the hidden creator middle class, platforms need to devote more resources to support a broader base of creators; and the creators can help themselves by capitalizing on community resources, seeking out education and training opportunities, and collaborating with each other.

CHAPTER 12

A New Hope

"The secret to getting ahead is getting started."

—MARK TWAIN, AUTHOR

Growing up in Paris, Alex Masmej longed to live out his dreams of moving to San Francisco and founding his own business. The 5,500 miles (nearly 9,000 kilometers) of distance was daunting enough, but the real barrier was the risky nature of becoming an entrepreneur.

With no resources, no money, and no network—just a small collective of a few thousand strangers following him on the internet—Alex didn't really see a straightforward way to pursue his dreams.

He first considered crowdfunding as the solution. According to financial marketplace Fundera, however, the average amount of money raised by all crowdfunding campaigns in 2021 was 824 dollars. This amount, even lower in 2020, was far from sufficient for Alex, so he decided to launch an unconventional experiment instead: he announced he would be offering the $ALEX social token in order to raise twenty thousand dollars.

A **social token**, as briefly mentioned in Chapter 8, is a type of cryptocurrency that allows a creator to monetize themselves through digital ownership. $ALEX, in his own words, is "a blend between a small Income Sharing Agreement and a human IPO." An investor who owns $ALEX tokens could help support Alex's dream in return for "owning" a small part of himself. Investors received 15 percent of all income he earned for the next three years, as well as special benefits such as having private one-on-one meetings with him and the ability to vote on Alex's day-to-day decisions (most of them being mundane tasks such as what he should eat that day).

As absurd as the idea was, $ALEX became a viral sensation. In turn, Alex surpassed his fundraising goal in five days.

For much of the book, we have discussed the appeal and advantages of the passion economy. We investigated how the passion economy improved upon the gig economy by allowing creators to monetize their individuality and cultivate an audience. Then, we took closer looks at how creators could unlock new opportunities and even earn a living.

As we have seen in the last two chapters, however, there are still many inequities creators (particularly the middle class of creators) face that are challenging for creator platforms to fully address and resolve. "In an era of platform-mediated work, network effects and platform data ownership lock creators into ecosystems that are often not designed to benefit their best interest," Li Jin shared with me in an interview.

The **ownership economy** seeks to address these issues and inequities by shifting distribution and ownership from platforms into the hands of individual consumers. As we saw with Alex, his community was eager to support his dreams. Following Alex on Twitter was just the beginning; investing directly in his future took things to a whole new level.

"There will always exist a power law, where massive creators like MrBeast or Jake Paul have a significantly larger audience than everyone else, but the floor of how much money you can make as a creator living off your passion is about to go up drastically. It will make creators more sustainable, where you don't need crazy amounts of money to live off your passion," Alex told me. Seeing how the passion economy is evolving to focus more on ownership, he posited, "I believe in a future where you don't have to be enslaved by an algorithm, sell merch, seek sponsorships, etc. Creators will be freer to be themselves."

Part III of this book has centered on Challenges and Opportunities. In the final chapter of this book, we discuss a new opportunity and direction the Creation Revolution is heading toward: the rise of the ownership economy.

●●●

When you think about what possessions you *own*, what comes to mind?

Perhaps your mind drifts to tangible products first, such as the rainbow-colored water bottle sitting at the corner of your desk, or the glossy smartphone currently slotted in your back pocket. When we consider a phone, however, we consider far more than the physical piece of metal and glass. A phone also entails digital assets such as data, photos, and messages.

Ownership is not just limited to palpable, materialistic items. Digital ownership and portability are equally important considerations, whether it entails *owning* a list of newsletter subscribers or *owning* a website domain to document your portfolio and resources. The more ownership of data, communication channels, content, and interactions that both creators and fans can have, the more power participants have over creator platforms.

Decentralization of ownership has risen as a natural result of the evolution of the World Wide Web over time. In its initial state, known as Web 1.0, online content was informational and read-only. In other words, internet users primarily were content consumers reading pieces of information on web pages. Publishing content online was needlessly difficult and costly. As a result, any online content you found on search engines was likely published by companies. There was very little support for user interaction or content generation.

Then, the rise of social networks and creator platforms brought about Web 2.0, where we are situated today. Users in Web 2.0 are granted the capacity to create content individually on large platforms and share their thoughts with internet users all around the world. However, the ownership of content and revenue still largely remains in the hands of centralized social platforms. For example, platforms like YouTube and tools like Patreon always take a cut of the creator's earnings.

The next stage, Web 3.0, is a decentralized web for users to share content and exchange money without the oversight of middlemen or intermediary institutions. The backbone of this decentralized web lies in the power of blockchain technology, and one specific application of blockchain in the real world is cryptocurrency (e.g., $ALEX).

"As the role of the *individual* in value creation becomes more commonplace, the next evolutionary step is towards software that is not only built, operated, and funded by individual users—but *owned* by users too," Variant Fund founder and investor Jesse Walden wrote.

The ownership economy, driven by the development of Web 3.0, thus has spun up a whirlwind of potential we are only just beginning to explore and unravel in terms of strengthening the creator-community relationships. We are moving toward a future where creators and fans can own and operate everything—their content, community, financial relationship, and businesses—themselves, just as we saw with Alex.

While some experts see a world where Web 3.0 entirely replaces Web 2.0, I envision a future where Web 3.0 supplements Web 2.0's functionalities—and that future is better than our current Web 2.0 system for both creators and fans.

As we saw in the last chapter, creator platforms prioritize and reward the top 1 percent of creators the most. By letting creators own their work, they can harness the collective impact of community and further drive their success without only waiting for a platform's algorithm to recommend their content. This way, Web 3.0 can empower creators who have built up a loyal audience (no matter how big or small) to succeed without depending on centralized platforms.

A creator and their community can thus transform into an interdependent and interlinked entity, with fans rewarded with an amount of tokens proportional to their excitement and value. Specifically, fans can gain tokens through monetary investments, or through demonstrating a history of fan engagement (potentially on Web 2.0 platforms, such as watching a creator's videos or commenting on their posts). In return, creators benefit from the shared exposure and focused engagement from their fan communities.

As a result, creators are no longer pitted against each other in a battle of recommendation algorithms and user attention. Instead, they can capitalize on their superfans to drive each creator's success forward without being at the expense of another's. Above all, this unlocks a new business model that is more sustainable for the creator middle class.

"The promise of the internet was to erase the gatekeepers. Instead of waiting for a record label to sign you, you could share your music on Spotify. Instead of asking a publication to share your words, you could tweet. Instead of being tapped by a studio exec, you could become a YouTuber. But what happened is that these platforms became the new gatekeepers," Index Ventures investor Rex Woodbury shared in *The Atlantic.* "The third era of the web is about righting the ship. Social capital becomes economic capital. Value no longer accumulates to brokers and intermediaries."

Social tokens, such as $ALEX, are only one of many innovations that have emerged with the rise of the ownership economy. NFTs and DAOs are two important tools that use social tokens:

- **Non-fungible tokens** (NFTs), a category of social tokens, are unique, irreplaceable units of data that represent pieces of digital media such as an image, video, audio, or art piece. NFTs are also built on top of blockchain technology, in order to establish and guarantee a verified and public proof of ownership. NFTs can be thought of as digital trading cards or rare collectibles. In 2022, Dune Analytics reported that the largest NFT marketplace, OpenSea, has over one million users who have made at least one transaction on the platform.

- **Decentralized autonomous organizations** (DAOs) are communities where their members control and operate the decision-making process rather than one centralized unit. For example, a creator can set up a DAO for their superfans. Fans can earn tokens to join the DAO by investing monetarily (e.g. buying an NFT) or demonstrating a history of fandom. Then, these fans can be further active stakeholders in the creator's work and initiatives.

A former influencer himself before becoming an investor and expert in this space, Rex has witnessed the pains and challenges of creators firsthand. "What we're seeing is that Web 3.0 can give creators a greater arsenal of tools. If used properly, Web 3.0 can unlock a lot of value," he said to me over the phone.

However, it is far from perfect, especially given how early we are in investigating the ups and downs of the ecosystem. A major source of concern is the extremely harmful environmental footprint of blockchain-dependent technologies. Cryptocurrencies such as Bitcoin and Ethereum, the latter of which most NFT marketplaces run on, are built on a system called "proof of work" that needs computers to solve complex math computations quickly in order to confirm secure transactions, thereby requiring intensive energy consumption. The unique insight that enables blockchain technology to provide secure decentralization is also its Achilles' heel.

For over fifteen years, French artist and climate activist Joanie Lemercier flew around the world to art fairs, galleries, and events to distribute and sell his art. Seeking more financially and environmentally sustainable alternatives, he discovered selling art as digital assets on the blockchain provided "secure ownership, traceability, artist commission on second market sales, and a thriving marketplace," bringing "a lot of benefits that the art market fails to provide." However, by the time he realized the disastrous environmental impact that blockchain technology caused, it was far too late. "[M]y release of six CryptoArt works consumed in ten seconds more electricity than [my] entire studio over the past two years," Joanie warned on his blog in early 2021.

To combat this pressing issue, technologists and scientists are working to develop more sustainable solutions.

For example, an alternative strategy to proof of work is the "proof of stake" system, where consumers stake tokens to verify a transaction rather than forcing computers to expend high amounts of energy. If Ethereum switches to a proof of stake model, then "Ethereum's electricity consumption will literally over a day or overnight drop to almost zero," Michel Rauchs, a research affiliate at the Cambridge Centre for Alternative Finance, told *The Verge*.

Today, artists are more cognizant about the environmental impact of NFTs. While some refuse to participate in this ecosystem entirely, others are optimistic about NFTs of the future growing more eco-friendly. A team of artists are leading GreenNFTs, an initiative offering bounties to anyone who develops new ways to improve the energy efficiency of the NFT economy. "Above all, we have faith in the ingenuity and creativity of the CryptoArt/NFT community and want to see it continue to flourish. Hopefully, this initiative is just the first of many as we continue to explore new ways to take ownership over the future of our creative economy in a way that is increasingly ecologically friendly and one we can be proud of," GreenNFTs's founder Jason Bailey stated on the initiative's website.

Furthermore, the novelty and hype surrounding Web 3.0 have made the space vulnerable to a slew of scams. For example, intriguing NFT projects have vanished as soon as the organizers finished collecting funds; these are known as "rugpulls," as if a rug has just been pulled out from under you.

Frosties, which rose to prominence in early 2022, is one such notable rugpull. An NFT art collection of adorable characters composed of ice cream scoops, Frosties had gathered forty thousand community members at its peak. One member, Joshua Christian, disclosed to technology publication *Protocol* that he spent about a thousand dollars on three Frosties. He was captivated not only by the art style, but also by the additional investment benefits promised by the Frosties organizers. Hours after the Frosties' public minting began, however, the community's Discord server disappeared. The scam left the community stunned; over 1.2 million dollars were stolen as a result, the funds moved in a series of quick transfers from Frosties' OpenSea wallet to other accounts.

"A lot of artists have never been paid fairly. Artists are often asked to do work for free or are underpaid and are told to be grateful. Our work isn't valued. You were a rich artist when you were dead. NFTs are changing that. Not only are we creating an environment wherein we're getting compensated fairly but we get a royalty on our work if it's resold," visual artist Jessica Ragzy Ewud (@ragzyart) told *Rolling Stone*. "This is why I hate all the scams and the rugpulls that have been happening, because I think it gives the space such a terrible name. What was meant to be so innovative and such a beautiful way for artists to finally capitalize on their work and ideas is now turning into a place with a lot of scams and negative things associated with it." As we enter this relatively uncharted territory, it is even more important to exercise caution as a creator or consumer.

Not only do additional infrastructures and tools need to be constructed with all ongoing learnings and issues in mind, more conversations—especially with a diverse range of creators and consumers—need to be held as we continue to design the next stage of the Creator Revolution *ethically and mindfully*. With technologies like social tokens and NFTs, which enable everything and everyone to become a potential investment, we toe the line of a *Black Mirror*-esque society where everything is monetized. "Financializing life and culture could distribute economic value more evenly and equitably, but the system must be designed with guardrails to ensure that we don't sacrifice our humanity," Rex emphasized in his writing.

For now, thankfully, it appears we have not fallen into that dystopian vision yet. In particular, the rise of community-driven technology gives creators a newfound ability to initiate more impact-oriented ventures.

Jade Darmawangsa, who we first met in Chapter 10, was nine years old when she uploaded a doll review video on YouTube, the first piece of content she ever published on the internet. Twelve years later, Jade is now a thriving fulltime creator with over 377,000 subscribers. She also serves as the CEO of influencer marketing agency X8 Media. While she still has continued to release videos on YouTube over the last decade, Jade has consistently explored new frontiers and businesses, her most recent venture being NFTree Haus.

How NFTree Haus works is that for every NFT they sell, NFTree Haus will plant a tree in urban and peri-urban environments. Owning an NFT from NFTree Haus provides the following benefits:

1. **Direct impact**: A tree is planted.
2. **Commitment**: As an owner, you have a stronger sense of belonging and commitment to helping the initiative succeed.
3. **Community membership**: The NFT grants entry to an environmental and climate-driven community.
4. **Community benefits**: The community shares resources and access to exclusive events.

5. **Democratized decision making**: You have the power to vote on future decisions NFTree Haus carries out.

"We want to generate impact through the power of creators, and we're using NFTs as a medium to fund these initiatives," Jade told me.

One of the most exciting prospects of the ownership economy is that by granting everyone access to ownership, any one of us can physically invest in creators or creator projects and reap the benefits as a community. As a result, this enables greater potential for more impact-driven community efforts that creators and their fans can organize together. For example, the elfDAO initiative harnessed blockchain technology and social tokens to successfully organize a holiday toy drive, donating tens of thousands of dollars to charities that the community sourced and voted on.

"I think in the next five years, creators will increasingly tap into Web3 technologies for social impact," Jade concluded.

Web 3.0 is a constantly evolving landscape that has both dogmatic support and vehement opposition. Insufficient regulation and underdeveloped infrastructure have resulted in risks like environmental concerns and large-scale scams, but its technology ultimately carries a lot of potential upsides for creators. That said, the ownership economy is not the only solution to the challenges we have probed in Part III. Instead, it opens up new avenues for creators to explore in addition to the many others mentioned throughout this book. I envision a future where Web 2.0 and Web 3.0 technologies coexist in complementary harmony.

Above all, I'm excited to see how we can all work together to better support creators and, to echo Jade's closing thoughts, empower society as a whole.

• • •

I began my content creation journey eight years ago as a wide-eyed high school kid who had no idea what she was getting herself into. I simply wanted to share the stories and ideas that were running through my head as writing and art with a few other online strangers.

A few became more than a few, and I discovered I was witnessing the beginnings of something incredible: the Creator Revolution.

Although I am no longer an active fiction or art creator (for the time being), today I create content about…creators. Very meta, I know. In writing this book, crafting my newsletter, and sharing insights on social media, I seek to share more stories about digital creators and the waves of impact they are imprinting on our society.

One of the most common questions I received during the writing process was, "Will your book still be relevant by the time you publish it?" It was every writer's biggest fear packed in an innocuous question. *Will your writing be relevant, or will it become obsolete? Will anyone still want to read it? Will people care enough to read it?*

To this, I have an easy answer for you: yes. This book has documented a pivotal period of history, from what led to the rise of creators, to the evolution of the passion economy, to the opportunities that being a creator can open up. It may appear that so much has progressed so quickly—and yet, perplexingly, we are still at the start of the Creator Revolution. From live commerce to the ownership economy, influencers to entrepreneurs, we are only seeing the beginning of a movement that will continue to transform and shape our daily lives.

As I interviewed creators, start-up founders, investors, and employees at creator platforms for this book, everyone I spoke with agreed on one key point: there has never been a better time to start being a creator.

The barriers to content creation are at an all-time low and will only continue to diminish. Furthermore, the path to becoming a creator is transforming into a more institutionalized path, starting at a young age. Throughout the book, we heard the stories of young creators like Ryan Kaji (who began at age three), TommyInnit (who began at age nine), and Macy Lee (who began at age fourteen). But it's not only for youths either: middle school teacher Claudine James, who we read about in Chapter 4, has soared into a TikTok star at age fifty-four; in China, ninety-three-year-old Niu Weina has grown into a national livestreaming sensation (Zhang, 2021). Current and future generations are learning from creators, what creators can achieve, and how to be a creator.

Perhaps you are afraid. Maybe you don't know what to create content about. Perhaps you're not even sure you belong as a creator.

But you do.

Because there is a consumption need for all kinds of content, creators have the ability to fit into every pocket of our society. Everything has a consumer, and thus everything, no matter how big or small, needs a creator. From comedy entertainment to dance tutorials to video gameplay to learning how to reset the password on those pesky luggage locks, content creation is required across all topics and will permeate through all sectors and industries.

"Being a content creator is fluid," YouTube creator and actress Prajakta Koli remarked to me. "There's no rhyme or rhythm to this. It's not compartmentalized." All types of content and creators are needed to continue building toward the Creator Revolution—and you can help join and grow this movement. There is no better time than the present to start creating.

From learning about larger societal shifts to various forms of self-made success, from inspecting the challenges and inequities that creators face to the potential solutions, you are now armed with insights and stories of how creators are transforming our present and our future.

Welcome to the Creator Revolution—I cannot wait to see what you create.

The Creator Revolution presents new opportunities in the form of the ownership economy. With tools like social tokens, NFTs, and DAOs, Web 3.0 has been touted as a potential solution to help address creator inequities, but it also carries risks and unforeseen consequences.

For more information, please visit

www.catherinehyeo.com/creator

Acknowledgments

Writing a book is by far the largest and most challenging project I have undertaken thus far. None of this would have been possible without the invaluable contributions of a number of incredibly supportive and thoughtful individuals.

First and foremost, I am eternally grateful for my family. From reading countless draft iterations to giving me advice on my most dejected nights, my mom and dad were as important to this book getting done as I was. There would be no book here today without your patience, time, and unwavering support, without you two encouraging your daughter to create and dream for a lifetime ahead. To my grandma, thank you for inspiring me at every step of the process. I would not be here today without you all and I am indescribably grateful.

Thank you to my dearest friends. Eric, the first person I told about my desire to write this book, believed in me from day one. You had a front-row seat to all the teeth gnashing, procrastination, and long nights, and you provided constant feedback and invaluable support throughout the entire journey. Jennifer and Megan, thank you for our boba trips and for carefully reading so many different parts of the book—you two sacrificed weekends and late nights to leave dozens of comments on a messy Google Doc. Justin and Audrey, thank you for taking the time to willingly comb through some of my worst writing and talk me through my scattered head of thoughts. To my writing buddies, Neha and Jenna, thank you for helping me stay sane and on track throughout our many intense writing sprints and "short" breaks—I cannot wait for both of your books to come out and have staked my spot as the first in line to buy them. To my six roommates, thank you for cheering me on throughout this past year. I am always touched when you all tone down the volume of *Mario Kart* to help me better focus writing on late Friday nights (including right now, as I am typing these exact words).

I had the unique opportunity to interview many outstanding people who have played pivotal roles in witnessing and growing the Creator Revolution. Thank you to all my interviewees for taking time out of your busy schedules to speak with me about your experiences, passions, and insights. Every conversation taught me something new and deepened my conviction for this book's need and my love for this space.

Many lengthy conversations and discussions helped shape my insights in profound ways while researching and writing this book. In particular, I want to thank Lila Shroff, Anita Ilango, and Luca Tomescu. I also want to acknowledge an intellectual debt to the experts and researchers whose trailblazing writings have inspired my interest and thinking in this space. Foremost among them are Li Jin, Taylor Lorenz, Kaya Yurieff, Scott Kominers, and Rex Woodbury. I am constantly learning from each and every one of you.

I cannot express enough gratitude for the amazing communities that have been faithful stalwarts of support over my many years as a creator and writer: my Tumblr friends, for spurring on high school Catherine to keep creating and sharing my artistic passions; the Writing Den, for inspiring me to start writing all these years ago—it has been my biggest joy seeing all of us grow and thrive as successful people and writers; Harvard's English department and Tuesday Magazine, for encouraging me to be unafraid and unashamed to show-case my words and voice; the Contrary family and We Are Family Foundation community, for rooting for me and my crazy endeavors/ideas each and every day; and my Twitter ecosystem, for helping support my book research and writing process and connecting me to so many wonderful new friends and collaborators. I also want to give special thanks to an important mentor who has had a huge influence on my writing journey throughout the years, my sixth-grade writing teacher Jennifer van Sijll. You were the first person who made me believe my writing was valuable enough to exist in the world.

This book would not be in your hands today without the support of my author community. Writing a book is a daunting journey, but the widespread support on my pre-order campaign validated my efforts and blew me away. I am so grateful to each of the following individuals who have been a part of this journey: Aibing Zhou, Aino Alkio, Alan Tu, Albert Shin, Alisha Sehgal, Ally Zhu, Alyssa Tang, Amanda Cheung, Ami Yoshimura, Ananya Anupam, Andrew Li, Andy Dent, Angela Chen, Anita Ilango, Anna Wang, Anson Yu, Anvisha Pai, April Chen, Ashley Wong, Athena Yeung, Audrey Shing, Bhagya Ram, Boon-Lock Yeo, Brittany Nickell, Cameron Akker, Cameryn Hodges, Carol W., Carolyn Ge, Cathy Williams, Charlotte Novy, Chenai Mangachena, Chuck See, Daran Wang, David Kobrosky, David Zeng, Dean Lizardo, Deborah Johnson, Denis Anisimov, Diana Voronin, Dylan Zhou, Elisée Djapa , Elizabeth Adams, Emilly Fan, Eric Koester, Eric Lin, Evelina Yeung, Frank Zhu, Grace Kwak, Haneul Shin, Hannah Cole, Hannah Lu, Helen Zhang, Hessie Jones, Hui She, Ilana Nguyen, Isabelle Zhou, Jack McClelland, Jacob Polatty, Jacqueline Kim, James Li, Jamie Roach, Jane

Zhang, Jared Smith, Jason Chen, Jeffrey Wang, Jenna Wang, Jennifer Guo, Jennifer He, Jennifer John, Jerry Registre, Jessica Li, Jessie Mindel, Jie Qu, Jieyun Wan, Jin Li, Joanna Teng, Jonathan Yuan, Jonathan Rosenberg, Joy Harjanto, Joy Yang, Ju Yon Kim, Junhua Duan, Justin Wong, Kacie Iuvara, Kara Ivancich, Karun Kaushik, Kathryn Tian, Katie Li, Kavya Kopparapu, Kemi Akenzua, Kevin King, Kok-Wui Cheong, Laura Murphy, Linda Qin, Lucas Wang, Manasi Maheshwari, Marie Williams, Mee-Jung Jang, Megan Yu, Memie Osuga, Michael Yan, Michael Zhang, Michele Wang, Minerva Yeung, Minli Virdone, Mohib Jafri, Nancy Lin, Neha Shukla, Penny Xia Gao, Pradyumna Shome, Rachel Hsin, Rae Jin, Ria Doshi, Ricky Grannis-Vu, Robert Gabel, Ryan Leung, Sayak Maity, Shriya Nevatia, Shuyi Tang, Sophia L., Tanishq Sandhu, Taryn Sumner, Theodor Sion, Tianjing Jiang, Victor Qin, Vivien Tran, Will Robbins, Woojin Lim, Xiang Gu, Yanyan Hu, Yash Dutt, Yu Ying, and Zev Nicolai-Scanio.

I cannot end this book without the biggest thank you of all: to the team at my publisher New Degree Press, especially Karina Agsibit, John Chancey, and Eric Koester, for helping turn my lifelong dream of writing a book into a reality.

Glossary

Burnout: A type of exhaustion caused by excessive and prolonged stress.

Creator (Digital content creator): Any individual who consistently publishes digital content and has built up an audience on an online platform(s).

Creator-market fit: The degree to which a creator meets strong audience (market) demand, a sustainable business model, and their own content creation goals. Achieving creator-market fit means you have reached the moment when all three components are satisfied.

Creator platform: Any platform that gives independent creators the ability to distribute their content and build a following. Examples include Instagram, Tumblr, YouTube, SoundCloud, Substack, and TikTok.

Creator tool: Any tool that assists independent creators, curators, and community builders, most often (but not limited to) helping them monetize their passion or scale their growth. Examples include Patreon, Canva, Beacons, Stir, and Rally.

Decentralized autonomous organization (DAO): A community in which its members control and operate the decision-making process rather than one central unit. To ensure transparency and decentralization, its financial transaction records and organizational rules are recorded on a blockchain.

Electronic commerce (e-commerce): The buying and selling of goods or services via the internet.

Gig economy: The system in which individuals engage in part-time work and are paid on a task-by-task basis. Ride-sharing apps, food/grocery delivery apps, and asset-sharing services are examples of gig economy marketplaces.

Influencer: Any individual who uses social media to grow a following and has the power to influence their audience's purchasing decisions in order to make money. Influencers are a subset of creators.

Knowledge creator: A type of content creator who focuses on sharing information about a specific topic(s) with the goal of educating/informing their audience.

Live commerce: A form of social commerce in which consumers watch live broadcast streams to discover new products, watch live product demos, and purchase the product.

Metaverse: A virtual world that exists beyond the one in which we live. The term does not refer to a specific type of technology, but instead points to a broader shift in how humans interact with technology.

Non-fungible token (NFT): A unique, irreplaceable unit of data that represents a piece of digital media, such as an image, video, audio, or art piece. NFTs are built on top of blockchain technology to establish and guarantee a verified and public proof of ownership.

Ownership economy: The system where all platforms will be built, operated, and owned by their users.

Parasocial relationship: A one-sided psychological attachment from a fan toward a high-profile figure (e.g., a creator).

Passion economy: The system of how individuals, especially content creators, can monetize their individuality and hobbies through unique, creative work.

Persona burnout: A type of burnout caused by the need to balance multiple personas and giving each persona their full energy and thought.

Serialized fiction: A format in which a single larger work of fiction is released and published in smaller installments.

Social commerce: A subset of e-commerce, social commerce transactions rely heavily on any form of online media that offers social interaction.

Social token: A type of cryptocurrency that allows a creator to monetize themselves through digital ownership.

Web 3.0: The evolution of the World Wide Web, as of now, is partitioned into three stages: Web 1.0, Web 2.0, and Web 3.0. Web 3.0 is the iteration of the web that is decentralized and self-governing. The vision for Web 3.0 is users can own and control their own data and actions on the internet.

Appendix

INTRODUCTION

Dzhanova, Yelena. "Forget Law School, These Kids Want to Be
a YouTube Star." *CNBC*, August 3, 2019. https://www.cnbc.
com/2019/08/02/forget-law-school-these-kids-want-to-be-a-
youtube-star.html.

James, Josh. "What 'Data Never Sleeps 9.0' Proves about the Pandemic." *Domosphere* (blog). *Domo,* October 4, 2021. https://
www.domo.com/blog/what-data-never-sleeps-9-0-proves-
about-the-pandemic.

Yuan, Yuanling, and John Constine. "SignalFire's Creator Economy Market Map." *SignalFire* (blog), 2020. https://signalfire.
com/blog/creator-economy.

CHAPTER 1

D'Anastasio, Cecilia. "Pokimane Has Done Enough—and Has So
Much Left to Do." *Wired*, August 26, 2021. https://www.wired.
com/story/pokimane-has-done-enough-and-has-so-much-
left-to-do.

Finley, Klint. "He Wanted a Unicorn. He Got…a Sustainable Business." *Wired*, January 19, 2020. https://www.wired.com/story/
he-wanted-unicorn-got-sustainable-business.

Jin, Li. "What Is the Definition of a 'Creator'? (As In, Creator Tools, Creator Economy, Etc)." *Li Jin* (blog), November 20, 2019. https://li-jin.co/2019/11/20/what-is-the-definition-of-a-creator-as-in-creator-tools-creator-economy-etc.

Lavingia, Sahil (@shl). "A bit different: someone who creates art and would create more art if they had more time/money." Twitter, November 20, 2019, 2:44 p.m. https://twitter.com/shl/status/1197284686164156421.

Lorenz, Taylor. "The Real Difference Between Creators and Influencers." *The Atlantic*, May 31, 2019. https://www.theatlantic.com/technology/archive/2019/05/how-creators-became-influencers/590725.

Online Etymology Dictionary. s.v. "Create." Accessed August 12, 2021, https://www.etymonline.com/word/create.

TikTok. "@caitlinnlam." Accessed February 20, 2022. https://www.tiktok.com/@caitlinnlam.

Twitch. "Pokimane." Accessed August 12, 2021. https://www.twitch.tv/pokimane.

YouTube. "Pokimane." Accessed August 12, 2021. https://www.youtube.com/c/pokimane/about.

CHAPTER 2

Antler (blog). "The Ultimate Guide to the Creator Economy." June 5, 2021. https://www.antler.co/blog/the-ultimate-guide-to-the-creator-economy.

Berg, Madeline. "How Nine-Year-Old Ryan Kaji, YouTube's $30 Million Man, Just Keeps Getting Richer." *Forbes*, December 18, 2020. https://www.forbes.com/sites/maddieberg/2020/12/18/how-nine-year-old-ryan-kaji-youtubes-30-million-man-just-keeps-getting-richer/?sh=47338e216c16.

MintLife (blog). Mint. "How Much Do Youtubers Make and How to Become a Youtuber." Last modified April 23, 2021. https://mint.intuit.com/blog/relationships/how-much-do-youtubers-make-5035.

@itssmithsonmichael. June 2, 2021. TikTok video, 0:52. https://www.tiktok.com/@itssmithsonmichael/video/6969235813603265797.

Jin, Li. "The Passion Economy and the Future of Work." a16z. October 8, 2019. https://a16z.com/2019/10/08/passion-economy.

Koetsier, John. "2 Million Creators Make 6-Figure Incomes On YouTube, Instagram, Twitch Globally." *Forbes*, October 5, 2020. https://www.forbes.com/sites/johnkoetsier/2020/10/05/2-million-creators-make-6-figure-incomes-on-youtube-instagram-twitch-globally.

Oxford Economics. *From Opportunity to Impact: Assessing the Economy, Societal and Cultural Benefits of YouTube in the US.* Oxford: 2020.

Patreon. "The Story of Patreon." Accessed January 18, 2022. https://www.patreon.com/about.

Rose, John, François Candelon, Dominic Field, Fang Ruan, and Qiuqing Tai. "'Bite-Sized' Videos Have a $193 Billion Economic

Footprint." Boston Consulting Group, March 2021. https://
web-assets.bcg.com/87/9b/1794e2644f21a40ee678fb3a2bab/
bcg-bite-sized-videos-have-a-193-billion-economic-footprint-
mar-2021.pdf.

Shapiro, Robert, and Siddhartha Aneja. *Taking Root: The
Growth of America's New Creative Economy*. Re:Create Coa-
lition: 2017. https://www.recreatecoalition.org/wp-content/
uploads/2019/02/ReCreate-2017-New-Creative-Economy-Study.
pdf.

Siberling, Amanda. "Tumblr Debuts Post+, a Subscription Service
for Gen Z Creators." *TechCrunch*, July 21, 2021. https://tech-
crunch.com/2021/07/21/tumblr-debuts-post-a-subscription-
service-for-gen-z-creators.

TED. "How Artists Can (Finally) Get Paid in the Digital Age |
Jack Conte." August 30, 2017. Video, 10:31. https://www.youtube.
com/watch?v=RlQ3C_VanaU.

Tseng, Ada. "How to Pay Your Bills When You're Starting Out in
Hollywood." *Los Angeles Times*, June 28, 2021. https://www.
latimes.com/entertainment-arts/business/story/2021-06-28/
hollywood-day-jobs-make-money-serving-tiktok-twitch.

U.S. Bureau of Labor Statistics. "Labor Force Statistics from the
Current Population Survey." January 22, 2021. https://www.bls.
gov/cps/cpsaat11.htm.

VidCon. "Be a Content Creator Like Chloe Ting." December 12,
2019. Video, 5:13. https://www.youtube.com/watch?v=urUBd-
1FRrvM.

Wertheimer, Linda. "Pomplamoose: Making a Living on YouTube."
April 9, 2010. NPR. Podcast, 9:48. https://www.npr.org/templates/story/story.php?storyId=125783271.

Yam, Sam, Li Jin, and Lauren Murrow. "a16z Podcast: How the Passion Economy Is Redefining Work." April 17, 2020. a16z. Podcast, 26:20. https://a16z.com/2020/04/17/passion-economy-pod.

YouTube. "Chloe Ting." Accessed February 17, 2022. https://www.youtube.com/c/ChloeTing/about.

Yurieff, Kaya. "Investments in Creator Economy Startups Hit $2 Billion; An Interview With Homebrew's Hunter Walk." *The Information*, June 23, 2021. https://www.theinformation.com/articles/investments-in-creator-economy-startups-hit-2-billion-an-interview-with-homebrew-s-hunter-walk.

CHAPTER 3

Arora, Arun, Daniel Glaser, Aimee Kim, Philipp Kluge, Sajal Kohli, and Natalya Sak. "It's Showtime! How Live Commerce Is Transforming the Shopping Experience." McKinsey & Company, July 21, 2021. https://www.mckinsey.com/business-functions/mckinsey-digital/our-insights/its-showtime-how-live-commerce-is-transforming-the-shopping-experience.

Berg, Madeline. "How Nine-Year-Old Ryan Kaji, YouTube's $30 Million Man, Just Keeps Getting Richer." *Forbes*, December 18, 2020. https://www.forbes.com/sites/maddieberg/2020/12/18/how-nine-year-old-ryan-kaji-youtubes-30-million-man-just-keeps-getting-richer/?sh=47338e216c16.

Bradley, Sydney. "How an Influencer Is Using TikTok and Instagram to Make Over $5,000 per Month after the Pandemic 'Ruined' Her Real-Estate Career." *Business Insider*, October 27, 2020. https://www.businessinsider.com/tiktok-skincare-influencer-makes-5000-per-month-with-affiliate-links-2020-10.

Contrera, Jessica. "When Every Moment of Childhood Can Be Recorded and Shared, What Happens to Childhood?" *The Washington Post*, December 7, 2016. https://www.washingtonpost.com/sf/style/2016/12/07/when-every-moment-of-childhood-can-be-recorded-and-shared-what-happens-to-childhood.

Drumm, Sarah. "What's Next for the Big Business of Influencer-Founded Brands?" *Thingtesting*, July 28, 2021. https://thingtesting.com/stories/influencer-founded-brands.

Geyser, Werner. "The State of Influencer Marketing 2020: Benchmark Report." *Influencer Marketing Hub*. Last updated February 14, 2021. https://influencermarketinghub.com/influencer-marketing-benchmark-report-2020.

Report Linker. "Global Social Commerce Industry." August, 2021. https://www.reportlinker.com/p05960121/Global-Social-Commerce-Industry.html.

Hallanan, Lauren. "Live Streaming Drives $6 Billion USD in Sales during the 11.11 Global Shopping Festival." *Forbes*, November 16, 2020. https://www.forbes.com/sites/laurenhallanan/2020/11/16/

live-streaming-drives-6-billion-usd-in-sales-during-the-1111-global-shopping-festival/?sh=2f16558721e5.

Hao, Karen. "Live-Streaming Helped China's Farmers Survive the Pandemic. It's Here to Stay." *MIT Technology Review*, May 6, 2020. https://www.technologyreview.com/2020/05/06/1001186/china-rural-live-streaming-during-cornavirus-pandemic.

Collective Bias. "Influencer Marketing Update: Non-Celebrity Influencers 10 Times More Likely to Drive In-Store Purchases." *PR Newswire*, March 29, 2016. https://www.prnewswire.com/news-releases/influencer-marketing-update-non-celebrity-influencers-10-times-more-likely-to-drive-in-store-purchases-300241060.html.

Dat, Trong. "Vietnam Could Make Billions of Us Dollars from Livestream Economy." VietNamNet News, July 21, 2021. https://vietnamnet.vn/en/feature/vietnam-could-make-billions-of-us-dollars-from-livestream-economy-757464.html.

Global Industry Analysts. "Global Social Commerce Industry." ReportLinker, August, 2021. https://www.reportlinker.com/p05960121/Global-Social-Commerce-Industry.html.

Huang, Alice. "Who Is Millionaire Li Jiaqi, China's 'Lipstick King' Who Raised More than US$145 Million in Sales on Singles' Day?" *South China Morning Post*, March 9, 2020. https://www.scmp.com/magazines/style/news-trends/article/3074253/who-millionaire-li-jiaqi-chinas-lipstick-king-who.

Huang, Zheping. "Could TikTok Jump into E-commerce?" *Bloomberg*, May 11, 2021. https://www.bloomberg.com/news/newsletters/2021-05-11/could-tiktok-jump-into-e-commerce.

Ifeanyi, KC. "This Startup Wants to Create a $400 Billion Live E-commerce Market in the U.S." *Fast Company*, February 10, 2022. https://www.fastcompany.com/90719391/this-startup-wants-to-create-a-400-billion-live-e-commerce-market-in-the-united-states.

Jennings, Rebecca. "TikTok Made Me Buy It." *Vox*, July 6, 2021. https://www.vox.com/the-goods/22555723/tiktok-viral-products-cerave-sky-high-mascara-amazon-leggings.

Kharif, Olga, and Matthew Townsend. "Livestreams Are the Future of Shopping in America." *Bloomberg*, September 14, 2020. https://www.bloomberg.com/news/features/2020-09-14/what-is-livestream-shopping-it-s-the-future-of-u-s-e-commerce.

Lebow, Sara. "Social Buyer Penetration Will Remain Highest in China This Year." *Insider Intelligence*, July 21, 2021. https://www.emarketer.com/content/social-buyer-penetration-remain-highest-china.

Lebow, Sara. "US Retail Social Commerce Will Reach Nearly $80 Billion by 2025." *Insider Intelligence*, August 17, 2021. https://www.emarketer.com/content/us-retail-social-commerce-will-reach-nearly-80-billion-by-2025.

Logan, Leah. "Are Celebrity Endorsements Worth the Money?" *Inmar Intelligence*, February 27, 2020. https://www.inmar.com/blog/thought-leadership/are-celebrity-endorsements-worth-money.

Lipsman, Andrew. "Social Commerce 2021: Media and Commerce Convergence Creates Growth Opportunity for Brands." *Insider Intelligence*, February 3, 2021. https://www.emarketer.com/content/social-commerce-2021.

Lorenz, Taylor. "The Real Difference Between Creators and Influencers." *The Atlantic*, May 31, 2019. https://www.theatlantic.com/technology/archive/2019/05/how-creators-became-influencers/590725.

Merriam-Webster Dictionary. s.v. "influencer (n.)." Accessed January 17, 2022, https://www.merriam-webster.com/dictionary/influencer.

Monteros, Maria. "What's Old Is New: Brands Craving Connection with Consumers Turn To Livestreaming." *Retail Dive*, May 19, 2021. https://www.retaildive.com/news/whats-old-is-new-brands-craving-connection-with-consumers-turn-to-livestr/600388.

Neate, Rupert. "Ryan Kaji, 9, Earns $29.5m as This Year's Highest-Paid Youtuber." *The Guardian*, December 18, 2020. https://www.theguardian.com/technology/2020/dec/18/ryan-kaji-9-earns-30m-as-this-years-highest-paid-youtuber.

Popper, Ben. "YouTube's Biggest Star Is a 5-Year-Old That Makes Millions Opening Toys." *The Verge*, December 22, 2016. https://www.theverge.com/2016/12/22/14031288/ryan-toys-review-biggest-youngest-youtube-star-millions.

Ryan's World. "Huge Eggs Surprise Toys Challenge with Inflatable Water Slide." April 13, 2016. Video, 5:57. https://www.youtube.com/watch?v=jjd-BeTX6Uo.

Shen, Xinmei. "Live-Streaming Sellers and Blockchain Engineers Are Officially Jobs in China Now." *South China Morning Post*, May 13, 2020. https://www.scmp.com/abacus/tech/article/3084264/live-streaming-sellers-and-blockchain-engineers-are-officially-jobs.

@thegerardoperez. December 12, 2020. Instagram video, 0:10. https://www.instagram.com/reel/CItMYrNn-M_.

@thegerardoperez. December 21, 2019. TikTok video, 0:09. https://www.tiktok.com/@thegerardoperez/video/6772890593887571205.

@thegerardoperez. November 15, 2020. TikTok video, 0:10. https://www.tiktok.com/@thegerardoperez/video/6895532575524244742.

Williams, Robert. "Gen Z Relies on Influencers for Purchase Decisions, Kantar Says." *Marketing Dive*, March 2, 2020. https://www.marketingdive.com/news/gen-z-relies-on-influencers-for-purchase-decisions-kantar-says/582890.

Xu, Selina. "Livestreaming Farmers Earn Millions from Fruit on China's TikTok." *Bloomberg*, July 7, 2021. https://www. bloomberg.com/news/articles/2021-07-07/livestreaming-farm-ers-earn-millions-from-fruit-on-china-s-tiktok.

YouTube. "Ryan's World." https://www.youtube.com/c/RyanToys-Review/about.

Yu, Cheng. "Livestreaming Bringing Online Sales to Life." *China Daily*, May 6, 2020. https://global.chinadaily.com. cn/a/202005/06/WS5eb21c5ca310a8b241153932_2.html.

CHAPTER 4

Bradshaw, Samantha, Hannah Bailey, and Philip N. Howard. *2020 Global Inventory of Organized Social Media Manipulation*. University of Oxford: 2020. https://demtech.oii.ox.ac.uk/wp-con-tent/uploads/sites/127/2021/02/CyberTroop-Report20-Draft9.pdf.

Criddle, Cristina. "Warning over 'Dangerous' DIY Beauty Trends on TikTok." *BBC News*, August 26, 2020. https://www.bbc.com/news/technology-53921081.

Dall'Asen, Nicola. "The 12 Best Makeup Tips We've Ever Learned From TikTok." *Allure*, April 24, 2020. https://www.allure.com/story/best-tiktok-makeup-tutorials.

DaveHax. "Ultimate Food Hacks Compilation" May 22, 2020. Video, 11:20. https://www.youtube.com/watch?v=VWUJQqljHzI.

Federal Trade Commission. "Advertising and Marketing." Accessed December 29, 2021. https://www.ftc.gov/tips-advice/business-center/advertising-and-marketing.

Gabrielle, Natasha. "Here's Why Gen Z Gets Its Investment Advice from Social Media." *The Ascent*, July 20, 2021. https://www.fool.com/the-ascent/buying-stocks/articles/heres-why-gen-z-gets-its-investment-advice-from-social-media.

Hiltzik, Michael. "Column: A Warning to Doctors—Spreading COVID Misinformation Could Cost You Your License." *Los Angeles Times*, August 16, 2021. https://www.latimes.com/business/story/2021-08-16/doctors-coronavirus-misinformation-license.

Jennings, Rebecca. "TikTok Made Me Buy It." *Vox*, July 6, 2021. https://www.vox.com/the-goods/22555723/tiktok-viral-products-cerave-sky-high-mascara-amazon-leggings.

Ogao, Emma. "Verified Twitter Users in Kenya Are Being Paid to Spread Disinformation." *Vice*, September 8, 2021. https://www.vice.com/en/article/xgx977/verified-twitter-users-in-kenya-are-being-paid-to-spread-disinformation.

Patel, Deep. "5 Differences between Marketing to Millennials VS. Gen Z." *Forbes*, November 27, 2017. https://www.forbes.com/sites/deeppatel/2017/11/27/5-d%E2%80%8Bifferences-%E2%80%8Bbe-tween-%E2%80%8Bmarketing-%E2%80%8Bto%E2%80%8B-m%E2%80%8Billennials-v%E2%80%8Bs%E2%80%8B-%E2%80%8Bgen-z/?sh=2a3bb502c9ff.

TikTok. "@iamthatenglishteacher." Accessed February 20, 2022. https://www.tiktok.com/@iamthatenglishteacher.

TikTok. "@rajyaatluri." Accessed February 20, 2022. https://www.tiktok.com/@rajyaatluri.

TikTok. "@vickichanmd." Accessed February 20, 2022. https://www.tiktok.com/@vickichanmd.

YouTube. "3Blue1Brown." Accessed February 20, 2022. https://www.youtube.com/c/3blue1brown/about.

YouTube. "Akili and Me." Accessed February 20, 2022. https://www.youtube.com/c/AkiliAndMe/about.

YouTube. "AsapScience." Accessed February 20, 2022. https://www.youtube.com/c/AsapSCIENCE/about.

YouTube. "CrashCourse." Accessed February 20, 2022. https://www.youtube.com/c/crashcourse/about.

YouTube. "Khan Academy." Accessed February 20, 2022. https://www.youtube.com/c/khanacademy/about.

CHAPTER 5

Abernathy, Penelope Muse. "The News Landscape in 2020: Transformed and Diminished." *US News Deserts*, 2020. https://www.usnewsdeserts.com/reports/news-deserts-and-ghost-newspapers-will-local-news-survive/the-news-landscape-in-2020-transformed-and-diminished.

Abram, Cleo (@cleoabram). "But over the last 2 years, I've started to feel a shift in the way we as a society cover things I care about: new tech that can profoundly change our world. We diminish it. We dismiss it. Before asking, in an intellectually honest way, if it worked, what could go right?" Twitter, January 10, 2022, 9:23 a.m. https://twitter.com/cleoabram/status/1480545957787885568.

Alter, Alexandra, and Elizabeth A. Harris. "What Snoop Dogg's Success Says about the Book Industry." *The New York Times*, last updated April 28, 2021. https://www.nytimes.com/2021/04/18/books/book-sales-publishing-pandemic-coronavirus.html.

Atkin, Emily (@emorwee). "Some personal news: Tomorrow is my last day @newrepublic! On Sept. 9, I'm launching a daily newsletter dedicated to original reporting + analysis on the climate crisis. It's called HEATED, and it would mean the world to me (literally) if you signed up:" Twitter, August 29, 2019, 3:34 p.m. https://twitter.com/emorwee/status/1167158669311696898.

Bauder, David. "Outlets Hurt by Dwindling Public Interest in News in 2021." *Associated Press News*, December 27, 2021. https://apnews.com/article/coronavirus-pandemic-health-business-presidential-elections-arts-and-entertainment-7cc91d-b0950a8e7e7bcf50d5d23dfc26.

Emmys. "Insecure." Accessed October 11, 2021. https://www.emmys.com/shows/insecure.

Errens, Julia. "ViacomCBS Takes Wattpad Stories to Streaming." December 22, 2021. https://www.stylus.com/viacomcbs-takes-wattpad-stories-to-streaming.

Griffin, Elle. "I'm Completely Changing My Newsletter Strategy This Year." *The Novelleist.* January 24, 2022. https://ellegriffin.substack.com/p/year-one.

Giorgis, Hannah. "How Issa Rae Built the World of *Insecure*." *The Atlantic*, December 24, 2021. https://www.theatlantic.com/culture/archive/2021/12/issa-rae-insecure-hbo-series-finale/621100.

Petersen, Anne Helen. "Some Personal News: Welcome to Culture Study." *Culture Study*, August 17, 2020. https://annehelen.substack.com/p/some-personal-news-welcome-to-culture.

Guduo. "骨朵热度指数排行榜 [Guduo Popularity Index Ranking]." Accessed February 21, 2022. https://d.guduodata.com.

Hua, Vanessa. "Awkward Stage." *Stanford Magazine*, May/June 2012. https://stanfordmag.org/contents/awkward-stage.

Instagram. "@kimsaira." Accessed December 29, 2021. https://www.instagram.com/kimsaira.

Jeong, Sarah. "Casey Newton on Leaving 'The Verge' for Substack and the Future of Tech Journalism." *OneZero*, September 23, 2020. https://onezero.medium.com/casey-newton-on-leaving-the-verge-for-substack-and-the-future-of-tech-journalism-974a646375fa.

Kantrowitz, Alex. "On Leaving BuzzFeed, and What's Next." *Big Technology*, May 26, 2020. https://bigtechnology.substack. com/p/on-leaving-buzzfeed-and-whats-next.

Kroll, Katy. "Read This before You See Work It." *Looper*, updated August 4, 2020. https://www.looper.com/231684/read-this-before-you-see-work-it.

Lutz, Ashley. "These 6 Corporations Control 90% Of the Media in America." *Business Insider*, June 14, 2012. https://www.businessinsider.com/these-6-corporations-control-90-of-the-media-in-america-2012-6.

McKenzie, Hamish. "What's Next for Journalists?" *On Substack*. May 18, 2020. https://on.substack.com/p/whats-next-for-journalists.

Payscale. "Average Journalist Salary." Accessed October 23, 2021. https://www.payscale.com/research/US/Job=Journalist/Salary.

Peabody Awards. "Insecure." Accessed October 11, 2021. https://peabodyawards.com/award-profile/insecure.

Rae, Issa. *The Misadventures of Awkward Black Girl.* 37 Ink, 2016.

Schlottman, Andrea. "The Serial Novel: A Brief History." *Books on the Wall* (blog). Accessed January 28, 2022. https://booksonthewall.com/blog/serial-novel-a-brief-history.

SimilarWeb. "Substack.com." Accessed January 28, 2022. https://www.similarweb.com/website/substack.com.

Taibbi, Matt. "Announcement to Readers: I'm Moving." *TK News*, April 6, 2020. https://taibbi.substack.com/p/announcement-to-readers-im-moving.

Tian, Ye. "网络文学市场规模超288亿元! 网文IP影视化改编成趋势? [The Scale of Online Literature Market Exceeds 28.8 Billion Yuan! Are Film and Television Adaptations of internet IP Film and Television Becoming a Trend?]." *Tencent News*, June 7, 2021. https://new.qq.com/omn/20210607/20210607A0AMCH00.html.

Tracy, Marc. "Journalists Are Leaving the Noisy internet for Your Email Inbox." *The New York Times*, September 23, 2020. https://www.nytimes.com/2020/09/23/business/media/substack-news-letters-journalists.html.

Valentine, Claire. "Tiktok Star 'Baby Ariel' Martin on Her New Film and Handling Cyberbullies." *Nylon*, February 19, 2020. https://www.nylon.com/baby-ariel-zombies-2-interview.

WarnerMedia. "WarnerMedia Extends Relationship with Issa Rae with Five-Year Overall Deal." March 24, 2021. https://press-room.warnermedia.com/vn/media-release/hbo-max/warner-media-extends-relationship-issa-rae-five-year-overall-deal.

Wei, He. "Online Reading Turns a Novel Business Opportunity as Digital Era Grows." *China Daily*, last updated May 14, 2021. http://www.chinadaily.com.cn/a/202105/14/WS609d-dc99a31024adobabde18.html.

CHAPTER 6

Brownlee, Dana. "How This Millennial Skipped Applications, Landed His Dream Tech Job Using Social Media." *Forbes*, February 7, 2021. https://www.forbes.com/sites/danabrownlee/2021/02/07/how-this-millennial-skipped-applications-landed-his-dream-tech-job-using-social-media.

Burgin, Ryder (*FootofaFerret*). "The History Of Domics (ft. Domics) | A Brief History." February 18, 2018. Video, 7:55. https://www.youtube.com/watch?v=OrMGKrXafEo.

Domics. "Domics: Rural." August 12, 2012. Video, 0:14. https://www.youtube.com/watch?v=H1iHoFrsbeo.

Greenwald, Michelle. "The Rise of Personal Brand Building from Execs to Creators and What You Need to Know to Get Started." *Forbes*, April 26, 2021. https://www.forbes.com/sites/michellegreenwald/2021/04/26/the-rise-of-personal-brand-building-from-execs-to-creators-and-what-you-need-to-know-to-get-started.

Lee, Joon. "The Yellow King." *The Ringer*, August 22, 2016. https://www.theringer.com/2016/8/22/16036670/the-kid-who-revolutionized-youtubes-tech-reviews-a5b9a2a03a04.

Lorenz, Taylor. "The Endless Stream." *The New York Times*, March 18, 2021. https://www.nytimes.com/2021/03/18/style/ludwig-ahgren-twitch-livestream.html.

Loyst, Meagan (@meaganloyst). "Any investors born '96 or later? I've been thinking a lot about Gen Z investing in Gen Z. Would love to compile key themes, fave co's, personal stories, etc.

with other Gen Z investors. Who should I chat with?" Twitter, October 1, 2020, 12:00 p.m. https://twitter.com/meaganloyst/status/1311697491201585152.

Marques Brownlee. "HP Pavilion dv7t Media Center Remote Overview." January 1, 2009. Video, 2:50. https://www.youtube.com/watch?v=9gk_rl3y_SU.

Marques Brownlee. "Update 1.0 = Video 100!" February 18, 2009. Video, 3:31. https://www.youtube.com/watch?v=FcugVUydSBY.

Merriam-Webster Dictionary. s.v. "passion (n.)." Accessed October 27, 2021, https://www.merriam-webster.com/dictionary/passion.

Ophelia, Alice. "Money Talks." *The Publish Press*, August 10, 2021. https://publishpress.substack.com/p/money-talks.

Panganiban, Dominic. (@domics). "Thinking 'bout starting a web comic. Maybe this'll be the first of many :]" Tumblr, August 22, 2010. https://domics.me/post/991892250/headspin.

Patel, Nilay. "The Business of Influence with MKBHD." *The Verge*, January 22, 2021. https://www.theverge.com/22231657/mkbhd-marques-brownlee-interview-youtube-creator-influencer-decoder.

Stephen, Bijan, and Jay Peters. "Ludwig Ends His 31-Day Stream by Breaking Ninja's All-Time Sub Record." *The Verge*, April 14, 2021. https://www.theverge.com/2021/4/14/22362532/ludwig-twitch-subathon-ends-stream-ninja-subs-record.

YouTube. "Domics." Accessed October 21, 2021. https://www.youtube.com/c/Domics/about.

YouTube. "Marques Brownlee." Accessed October 9, 2021. https://www.youtube.com/c/mkbhd/about.

CHAPTER 7

Chen, Tanya. "A College Student behind a Massively Popular Paint-Mixing TikTok Page Was Fired from Sherwin-Williams." *BuzzFeed News*, November 18, 2020. https://www.buzzfeednews.com/article/tanyachen/college-student-behind-a-massively-popular-paint-mixing.

Glamour. "YouTube Makeup Guru Michelle Phan on Becoming a Beauty Superstar: 'My Only Goal Was to Help My Family.'" September 3, 2013. https://www.glamour.com/story/michelle-phan-youtube-beauty-glamour-october-2013.

Griffith, Erin. "YouTube Star Michelle Phan's Beauty Startup Ipsy Raises $100 Million." *Fortune Magazine*, September 14, 2015. https://fortune.com/2015/09/14/ipsy-glam-bag-michelle-phan-funding.

Hou, Kathleen. "Michelle Phan Was YouTube's Biggest Beauty Star. Then She Vanished." *The Cut*, September 26, 2019. https://www.thecut.com/2019/09/michelle-phan-youtube-beauty-star-on-why-she-left.html.

Lukas, Erin. "Why Michelle Phan Will Always Take a Sweatpants Approach to Makeup." *InStyle*, August 4, 2021. https://www.

instyle.com/beauty/makeup/michelle-phan-em-cosmetics-interview.

Lunden, Ingrid. "LinkedIn Launches a $25m Fund for Creators, Will Test Clubhouse-Style Audio Feature in Coming Weeks." *TechCrunch*, September 14, 2021. https://techcrunch.com/2021/09/14/linkedin-is-launching-its-own-25m-fund-and-incubator-for-creators.

Merriam-Webster Dictionary. s.v. "entrepreneur (n.)." Accessed September 27, 2021. https://www.merriam-webster.com/dictionary/entrepreneur.

Michelle Phan. "Natural Looking Makeup Tutorial." May 20, 2007. Video, 7:09. https://www.youtube.com/watch?v=OB8nfJCOIeE.

Morris, Alex. "Michelle Phan: The Beauty Director." *New York Magazine*, April 18, 2014. https://nymag.com/news/media/internet-fame/michelle-phan-2014-4.

The Publish Press. "Creator Q&A: Tonester Paints." December 10, 2021. https://publishpress.substack.com/p/tonester.

@tonesterpaints. December 14, 2019. TikTok video, 0:11. https://www.tiktok.com/@tonesterpaints/video/6770383964742962438.

TikTok. "@tonesterpaints." Accessed December 29, 2021. https://www.tiktok.com/@tonesterpaints.

Twitch. "Frequently Asked Questions." https://www.twitch.tv/p/en/partners/faq.

Weiss, Geoff. "Michelle Phan's Latest Startup Helps Creators Find Free Music for Their YouTube Videos." *Tubefilter*, June 28, 2018.

Wick, Krista. "Meet Michelle Phan, the Accidental Millionaire." *The Insider*, May 17, 2012. Archived at https://web.archive.org/web/20140217030735/http://theinsider.etonline.com/gossip/52419_Michelle_Phan_The_Accidental_Millionaire.

YouTube. "Michelle Phan." Accessed July 23, 2021. https://www.youtube.com/c/MichellePhan/about.

YouTube. "Nastassia Ponomarenko." Accessed August 20, 2021. https://www.youtube.com/c/NastassiaPonomarenko/about.

YouTube. "Tonester Paints." Accessed December 29, 2021. https://www.youtube.com/c/TonesterPaints/about.

CHAPTER 8

Animal Capital. Accessed December 20, 2021. https://www.animalcapital.co.

Barber, Kayleigh. "No Longer under BuzzFeed, the Try Guys Are Building an Independent Media Business." *Digiday*, December 16, 2019. https://digiday.com/future-of-tv/no-longer-buzzfeed-try-guys-building-independent-media-business.

Beast Philanthropy. "Who We Are." Accessed February 1, 2022. https://www.beastphilanthropy.org/about.

BuzzFeedVideo. "The Try Guys Try Drag For The First Time." December 7, 2014. Video, 8:48. https://www.youtube.com/watch?v=7f-gCfC3bMoU.

Doyle, Hannah. "F**k That's Delicious." *The Publish Press*, February 1, 2022. https://publishpress.substack.com/p/fk-thats-delicious.

Jin, Li (@ljin18). "Creator-market fit is the union between content creation, audience, and business model. - Content: "Do I enjoy making this?" - Audience: "Do people want this?" - Business model: "Can I sustain myself?" Creator economy companies: which part(s) of this are you indispensable for?" Twitter, March 29, 2021, 12:40 a.m. https://twitter.com/ljin18/status/1376393732610785283.

Leiber, Sarah Jae. "Food Network Strikes New Deal With the Try Guys." *BroadwayWorld*, February 24, 2021. https://www.broadwayworld.com/bwwtv/article/Food-Network-Strikes-New-Deal-With-The-Try-Guys-20210224.

Lessin, Sam. "Equity Financing for Influencers." *The Information*, January 26, 2021. https://www.theinformation.com/articles/equity-financing-for-influencers.

Lessin, Sam. "'MrBeast' Explains His Plans to Help YouTube Creators Raise Equity Finance." *The Information*, March 24, 2021. https://www.theinformation.com/articles/mrbeast-explains-his-plans-to-help-youtube-creators-raise-equity-finance.

Loizos, Connie. "Jake Paul Looks to Knock Out the Venture Capital World with Anti Fund." *TechCrunch*, March 29, 2021. https://techcrunch.com/2021/03/29/jake-paul-looks-to-knock-out-the-venture-capital-world-with-anti-fund.

MrBeast. "I Counted to 100,000!" January 8, 2017. Video, 23:48:05. https://www.youtube.com/watch?v=xWcldHxHFp0.

Pokimane (@pokimanelol). "it's so surreal to say this but.. i've officially invested in theragun/therabody alongside absolute LEGENDS like rihanna, kevin durant, shawn mendes, justin timberlake, and more.. !! is this real life." Twitter, April 10, 2021, 3:33 p.m. https://twitter.com/pokimanelol/status/1380967272777359362.

Perez, Sarah. "Teen Banking Service Step Raises $50m, Adds Tiktok Star Charli D'Amelio to Investor List." *TechCrunch*, December 2, 2020. https://techcrunch.com/2020/12/02/teen-banking-service-step-raises-50m-adds-tiktok-star-charli-damelio-to-investor-list.

Shaw, Lucas, and Mark Bergen. "The North Carolina Kid Who Cracked YouTube's Secret Code." *Bloomberg*, December 22, 2020. https://www.bloomberg.com/news/articles/2020-12-22/who-is-mrbeast-meet-youtube-s-top-creator-of-2020.

Spangler, Todd. "Esports Firm 100 Thieves Worth $460 Million after Raising $60 Million in Funding." *Variety*, December 2, 2021. https://variety.com/2021/digital/news/100-thieves-valuation-60-million-funding-1235124640.

Sun, Rebecca. "Why YouTube Megastar KevJumba Mysteriously Disappeared." *The Hollywood Reporter*, August 28, 2017. https://www.hollywoodreporter.com/news/general-news/why-kevjumba-disappeared-inside-youtube-stars-departure-1031552.

Wojcicki, Susan. "Letter from Susan: Our 2021 Priorities." *YouTube Official Blog*, January 26, 2021. https://blog.youtube/inside-youtube/letter-from-susan-our-2021-priorities.

YouTube. "joycebean." Accessed January 31, 2022. https://www.youtube.com/c/joycebean/about.

YouTube. "MrBeast." Accessed February 1, 2022. https://www.youtube.com/c/MrBeast6000/about.

YouTube. "Try Guys." Accessed October 7, 2021. https://www.youtube.com/c/tryguys/about.

CHAPTER 9

Brown, Abram, and Abigail Freeman. "The Highest-Paid YouTube Stars: MrBeast, Jake Paul and Markiplier Score Massive Paydays." *Forbes*, January 14, 2022. https://www.forbes.com/sites/abrambrown/2022/01/14/the-highest-paid-youtube-stars-mrbeast-jake-paul-and-markiplier-score-massive-paydays/?sh=286e07721aa7.

Brown, Eileen. "Americans Spend Far More Time on Their Smartphones than They Think." *ZDNet*, April 28, 2019. https://www.zdnet.com/article/americans-spend-far-more-time-on-their-smartphones-than-they-think.

GLAAD. "Overview of Findings." 2020. https://www.glaad.org/sri/2020/overview.

GLAAD Media Institute. "Where We Are on TV: 2020-2021." Accessed January 27, 2022. https://www.glaad.org/sites/

default/files/GLAAD%20-%20202021%20WHERE%20WE%20
ARE%20ON%20TV.pdf.

Hawk, Crystal Echo. "Indigenous Representation Is Still Scarce in Hollywood: 'We Need More Native Stories'." *Variety*, October 11, 2021. https://variety.com/2021/film/opinion/indigenous-representation-hollywood-native-stories-1235086445.

Hoang, Kristie-Valerie. "'I Didn't Need to Apologize for Being Asian:' since Its Start, YouTube Allowed Creators to Celebrate Asian Joy." *Insider*, June 3, 2021. https://www.insider.com/youtube-asian-representation-wongfu-nigahia-michellephan.

Instagram. "@corpusren." Accessed January 7, 2022. https://www.instagram.com/corpusren.

Instagram. "#lgbtq." Accessed January 12, 2022. https://www.instagram.com/explore/tags/lgbtq.

Instagram. "@pinkmantaray." Accessed November 12, 2021. https://www.instagram.com/pinkmantaray.

Jenna Wang. "[High School Dance In-Public] "Swalla" - Blackpink Lisa Solo Dance (Kpop in Public Challenge)." February 10, 2019. Video, 2:18. https://www.youtube.com/watch?v=3dON-HCZ11To.

Kassel, Gabrielle. "Media Lacks Queer Representation—So Gen Z Is Turning to TikTok for Change." *HelloGiggles*, August 26, 2021. https://hellogiggles.com/lifestyle/tiktok-gen-z-lgbtq-community.

Mineo, Liz. "Schuyler Bailar Races toward His Authentic Self." *The Harvard Gazette*, May 15, 2019. https://news.harvard.edu/gazette/story/2019/05/ncaas-first-openly-transgender-swim-mer-schuyler-bailar-finds-his-real-self-and-flourishes-at-har-vard.

Miranda, Gabriela. "'I Became What I Didn't See': Latinx and Hispanic Influencers Speak Up about Representation." *USA Today*, October 13, 2021. https://www.usatoday.com/story/news/nation/2021/10/13/black-and-asian-latinx-influencers-dis-cuss-lack-representation/5841437001.

TED. "The Danger of a Single Story | Chimamanda Ngozi Adi-chie." October 7, 2009. Video, 19:16. https://www.youtube.com/watch?v=D9Ihs241zeg.

Thao, Phillipe. "Before 'Crazy Rich Asians,' Youtubers Paved the Way for Better Asian Representation." *Teen Vogue*, August 15, 2019. https://www.teenvogue.com/story/youtube-asian-repre-sentation-wongfuproductions-happyslip.

USC Annenberg. "Inequality in 1,300 Popular Films: Examining Portrayals of Gender, Race/Ethnicity, LGBTQ & Disability from 2007 to 2019." September 8, 2020. https://assets.uscan-nenberg.org/docs/aii-inequality_1300_popular_films_09-08-2020.pdf.

Whittenburg, Zachary. "How Online Videos Changed Dance." *Dance Magazine*, 2018. https://www.dancemagazine.com/how-online-videos-changed-dance-2518906563.html.

Woodbury, Rex. "What People Misunderstand about the Creator Economy." *Digital Native*, March 24, 2021. https://digitalnative. substack.com/p/what-people-misunderstand-about-the.

YouTube. "Jenna Wang." Accessed July 14, 2021. https://www.youtube.com/c/JennaWangOfficial/about.

CHAPTER 10

American Psychological Association. "Stress in America™ Generation Z." October 2018. https://www.apa.org/news/press/releases/stress/2018/stress-gen-z.pdf.

AnthonyPadilla. "I Spent a Day with Minecrafters (TommyInnit, Ranboo, Nihachu)." May 21, 2021. Video, 20:42. https://www.youtube.com/watch?v=_9JiBWwW3VE.

Carman, Ashley. "Fake Instagrams Are One of the Last Refuges of the Authentic Online Self." *The Verge*, last updated April 5, 2018. https://www.theverge.com/2018/4/3/17189912/fake-instagram-finsta-account-whyd-you-push-that-button.

Cook, Jesselyn. "Female Twitch Streamers Spend Their Lives Online. Predators Are Watching." *The Huffington Post*, July 20, 2021. https://www.huffpost.com/entry/female-twitch-streamers-sexual-harassment_n_60e8ab3ee4b06dfc5e215f54.

Davey, Lizzie. "Why Consistency in Content Creation Is So Important: An Interview with The858." *Tint* (blog), February 1, 2017. https://www.tintup.com/blog/consistency-content-creation-important-interview-the858.

Dendy, Michelle. "Friend: Shooter Had Fixation on 'The Voice' Singer." *News 6 WKMG | ClickOrlando*, June 22, 2016. https://www.clickorlando.com/news/2016/06/22/friend-shooter-had-fixation-on-the-voice-singer.

Dolph, Sam. "Interview with LGBTQ YouTube Star Shannon Beveridge." *Teen Vogue*, June 19, 2017. https://www.teenvogue.com/story/shannon-beveridge-youtube-star.

Farokhmanesh, Megan. "YouTubers Are Not Your Friends." *The Verge*, September 17, 2018. https://www.theverge.com/2018/9/17/17832948/youtube-youtubers-influencer-creator-fans-subscribers-friends-celebrities.

International Labour Organization. "ILO: Uncertain and Uneven Recovery Expected Following Unprecedented Labour Market Crisis." January 25, 2021. https://www.ilo.org/global/about-the-ilo/newsroom/news/WCMS_766949/lang--en/index.htm.

Istein, Linda Stein. "Suspected Stalker from Michigan Shows up at Radnor Teenager's House." *Delaware County Daily Times*, last updated June 25, 2021. Archived at https://web.archive.org/web/20210825094633/https://www.delcotimes.com/news/suspected-stalker-from-michigan-shows-up-at-radnor-teenager-s/article_a2e08e3c-c5a2-5b92-b3ed-238f3c2cccf3.html.

Jennings, Rebecca. "The Influencers Are Burned Out, Too." *Vox*, May 25, 2021. https://www.vox.com/the-goods/2021/5/25/22451987/influencer-burnout-tiktok-clubhouse.

LinkedIn. "Nick Singh." Accessed February 5, 2022. https://www.linkedin.com/in/nipun-singh.

Lorenz, Taylor. "Young Creators Are Burning Out and Breaking Down." *The New York Times*, last updated September 17, 2021. https://www.nytimes.com/2021/06/08/style/creator-burnout-social-media.html.

OfflineTV Podcast. "Nigahiga: Twitch Streamer ft. Ryan Higa | OfflineTV Podcast #28." July 26, 2020. Video, 1:04:58. https://www.youtube.com/watch?v=INcFLUiGd9Q.

Paiella, Gabriella. "Olivia Rodrigo Was Built 4 This." *GQ*, August 4, 2021. https://www.gq.com/story/olivia-rodrigo-profile.

Patchin, Justin W. "New National Bullying and Cyberbullying Data." Cyberbullying Research Center, October 10, 2016. https://cyberbullying.org/new-national-bullying-cyberbullying-data.

Rideout, Victoria, Susannah Fox, Alanna Peebles, and Michael B. Robb. "Coping with COVID-19: How Young People Use Digital Media to Manage Their Mental Health." San Francisco, CA: Common Sense and Hopelab, 2021. https://assets.hopelab.org/wp-content/uploads/2021/03/2021-coping-with-covid19-full-report.pdf.

Skinner, Paige. "YouTube's Biggest Stars Are Begging Fans Not to Stalk Them at Home." *The Daily Beast*, January 23, 2020. https://www.thedailybeast.com/youtube-stars-like-david-dobrik-and-colleen-ballinger-are-begging-fans-not-to-stalk-them-at-home.

Swanson, Barrett. "The Anxiety of Influencers." *Harper's Magazine*, June 2021. https://harpers.org/archive/2021/06/tiktok-house-collab-house-the-anxiety-of-influencers.

Twitch. "QTCinderella." Accessed February 25, 2022. https://www.twitch.tv/qtcinderella.

Vibely. "Creator Burnout Report." Accessed February 25, 2022. https://www.vibely.io/creator-burnout-report.

Weiss, Suzannah. "6 YouTube Celebs Speak Out on Cyberbullying." *Teen Vogue*, February 21, 2018. https://www.teenvogue.com/gallery/youtubers-open-up-about-cyberbullying.

YouTube. "Cameryn Grace." Accessed February 5, 2022. https://www.youtube.com/c/CamerynGrace/about.

Zhong, Tiffany, and Connie Chan. "Designing For, Marketing To, and Partnering with Gen Z." October 19, 2020, *a16z Future*. Podcast, 32:59. https://future.a16z.com/podcasts/decoding-gen-z.

CHAPTER 11

Asare, Janice Gassam. "Does TikTok Have a Race Problem?" *Forbes*, April 14, 2020. https://www.forbes.com/sites/janice-gassam/2020/04/14/does-tiktok-have-a-race-problem/?sh=2ccofbc93260.

Bentley, Elliot, and Kyle Kim. "Twitch Streamer Earnings Increase for Top Gamers, Data from Hack Shows." *The Wall Street Journal*, October 9, 2021. https://www.wsj.com/articles/

twitch-streamer-earnings-increase-for-top-gamers-data-from-hack-shows-11633802185.

Doyle, Hannah. "Prime Time." *The Publish Press*, January 7, 2022. https://publishpress.substack.com/p/primetime.

Fischer, Sara. "The Podcast Business Is Booming, but Few Are Making Money." *Axios*, January 25, 2021. https://www.axios.com/podcast-business-booming-few-making-money-d56001ob-538f-472f-bf9d-3ea8deb97488.html.

Fischer, Sara. "Pandemic Spurs Journalists to Go It Alone via Email." *Axios*, September 24, 2020. https://www.axios.com/pandemic-spurs-journalists-to-go-it-alone-via-email-613ca2d5-e8d5-4235-9582-48cc028e9d8b.html.

Garcia, Ethan. "OfflineTV signs Masayoshi, QuarterJade, and Sydeon." *Dot Esports*, November 19, 2021. https://dotesports.com/streaming/news/offlinetv-signs-masayoshi-quarter-jade-and-sydeon.

Google. "Google for Creators." Accessed October 21, 2021. https://blog.google/google-for-creators.

Gumroad. "Last Year in the Creator Economy." January 12, 2021. https://gumroad.gumroad.com/p/last-year-in-the-creator-economy.

Hong, James, and David Jang. "[A Deep Discussion with Scarra] Scarra Reveals His Thoughts on DL vs qt, Harry Potter, and Offlinetv." *Inven Global*, September 25, 2018. https://www.

invenglobal.com/articles/6205/a-deep-discussion-with-scarra-scarra-reveals-his-thoughts-on-dl-vs-qt-harry-potter-and-offlinetv.

Ingham, Tim. "Spotify Dreams of Artists Making a Living. It Probably Won't Come True." *Rolling Stone*, August 3, 2020. https://www.rollingstone.com/pro/features/spotify-million-artists-royalties-1038408.

Jin, Li. "The Creator Economy Needs a Middle Class." *Harvard Business Review*, December 17, 2020. https://hbr.org/2020/12/the-creator-economy-needs-a-middle-class.

Lorenz, Taylor. "Hype House and the Los Angeles TikTok Mansion Gold Rush." *The New York Times*, updated May 21, 2020. https://www.nytimes.com/2020/01/03/style/hype-house-los-angeles-tik-tok.html.

Means of Creation. "Taylor Lorenz on the Creator Economy, Online Entrepreneurship, the Changing Media Landscape, & More." October 24, 2020. Video, 52:32. https://www.youtube.com/watch?v=T9ZI4MJPEJA.

On Substack. "Building a Team to Help Writers Flourish." June 14, 2021. https://on.substack.com/p/building-a-team-to-help-writers-flourish.

Pinterest. "Your Ideas Belong Here: Apply for the Creator Fund." Accessed February 7, 2022. https://business.pinterest.com/en/blog/apply-pinterest-creator-fund.

Santalo, Andrei. "LinkedIn's Latest Investment in Creators." LinkedIn, September 14, 2021. https://www.linkedin.com/pulse/linkedins-latest-investment-creators-andrei-santalo.

Shirky, Clay. "Power Laws, Weblogs, and Inequality." *Clay Shirky's Writings About the internet* (blog), last updated February 10, 2003. Archived at https://web.archive.org/web/20040707084914/http://www.shirky.com/writings/powerlaw_weblog.html.

Substack. "Introducing Substack Bridge." Accessed October 21, 2021. https://substack.com/bridge.

Woodbury, Rex. "An Interview with OnlyFans Creator Jasmine Rice." *Digital Native*, February 3, 2021. https://digitalnative.substack.com/p/an-interview-with-onlyfans-creator.

Wu, Carolina. "Ruhnn: Blogger Incubators Disrupt China's Ecommerce Industry." *Parklu*, September 14, 2017. https://www.parklu.com/ruhan-blogger-incubators-china-ecommerce.

Wylde, Kaitlyn. "What Happened When Jasmine Rice Put a Paywall on Her Tweets." *Bustle*, last updated March 31, 2021. https://www.bustle.com/life/jasmine-rice-fanhouse-cofounder-onlyfans-pandemic.

YouTube. "Amal Elmziryahi." Accessed February 7, 2022. https://www.youtube.com/c/amalyabb/about.

YouTube. "درama كوين [Drama Queen]." Accessed February 7, 2022. https://www.youtube.com/c/DramaQueen/about.

YouTube. "JaySajer." Accessed February 7, 2022. https://www.youtube.com/c/JaySajer/about.

YouTube. "OfflineTV." Accessed February 7, 2022. https://www.youtube.com/c/OfflineTVgg/about.

YouTube. "Miva Flowers." Accessed February 7, 2022. https://www.youtube.com/c/MivaFlowers/about.

CHAPTER 12

Artnome. "GreenNFTs." Accessed February 14, 2022. https://www.artnome.com/greennfts.

Calma, Justine. "The Climate Controversy Swirling around NFTS." *The Verge*, March 15, 2021. https://www.theverge.com/2021/3/15/22328203/nft-cryptoart-ethereum-blockchain-climate-change.

Dune Analytics. "Total OpenSea traders over time (Ethereum)." Accessed February 14, 2022. https://dune.xyz/queries/2877/5680.

elfDAO. "Santa's Not Real, but His Elves Are." Accessed February 26, 2022. https://elfdao.com.

Hissong, Samantha. "NFT Scams Are Everywhere. Here's How to Avoid Them." *Rolling Stone*, January 24, 2022. https://www.rollingstone.com/culture/culture-features/nft-crypto-scams-how-to-not-get-scammed-1286614.

Lemercier, Joanie. "The Problem of (Ethereum) CryptoArt." *Studio Joanie Lemercier* (blog), February 17, 2021. https://joanielemercier.com/the-problem-of-cryptoart.

Masmej, Alex. "Taking Risks during Chaos: Initial $ALEX Offering." *Medium*, April 7, 2020. https://medium.com/@AlexMasmej/taking-risks-during-chaos-initial-alex-offering-339883bb7f6d.

Pimentel, Benjamin. "Anatomy of an NFT Art Scam: How the Frosties Rug Pull Went Down." *Protocol*, February 24, 2022. https://www.protocol.com/fintech/frosties-nft-rug-pull.

Shepherd, Maddie. "Crowdfunding Statistics: Market Size and Growth." Fundera. Last updated December 16, 2020. https://www.fundera.com/resources/crowdfunding-statistics.

Walden, Jesse. "The Ownership Economy: Crypto & the Next Frontier of Consumer Software." Variant Fund, July 14, 2020. https://variant.fund/writing/the-ownership-economy-crypto-and-consumer-software.

Woodbury, Rex. "What Happens When You're the Investment." *The Atlantic*, November 29, 2021. https://www.theatlantic.com/ideas/archive/2021/11/financialization-everything-investment-system-token/620804.

YouTube. "Jade Darmawangsa." Accessed February 12, 2022. https://www.youtube.com/c/jadedarmawangsa/about.

Zhang, Binjing. "师从梁思成的93岁清华奶奶直播讲宋词走红: 我这是' 逆生长' [The 93-Year-Old Tsinghua Grandmother Who Studied under Liang Sicheng's Live Broadcast of Song Poetry Became Popular: I Am 'Reverse Growth']." *Tsinghua Alumni Association*, October 28, 2021. https://www.tsinghua.org.cn/info/1014/36137.htm.